I0015452

SQL Server 2014 Development Essentials

Design, implement, and deliver a successful database
solution with Microsoft SQL Server 2014

Basit A. Masood-Al-Farooq

BIRMINGHAM - MUMBAI

SQL Server 2014 Development Essentials

Copyright © 2014 Packt Publishing

All rights reserved. No part of this book may be reproduced, stored in a retrieval system, or transmitted in any form or by any means, without the prior written permission of the publisher, except in the case of brief quotations embedded in critical articles or reviews.

Every effort has been made in the preparation of this book to ensure the accuracy of the information presented. However, the information contained in this book is sold without warranty, either express or implied. Neither the author, nor Packt Publishing, and its dealers and distributors will be held liable for any damages caused or alleged to be caused directly or indirectly by this book.

Packt Publishing has endeavored to provide trademark information about all of the companies and products mentioned in this book by the appropriate use of capitals. However, Packt Publishing cannot guarantee the accuracy of this information.

First published: July 2014

Production reference: 1180714

Published by Packt Publishing Ltd.
Livery Place
35 Livery Street
Birmingham B3 2PB, UK.

ISBN 978-1-78217-255-0

www.packtpub.com

Cover image by Angela Robledo (angel.spo@gmail.com)

Credits

Author
Basit A. Masood-Al-Farooq

Reviewers
Basavaraj Biradar
Brenner Grudka Lira
David Loo
Richard Louie
José (Cheo) Redondo

Acquisition Editor
Neha Nagwekar

Content Development Editor
Neil Alexander

Technical Editor
Pankaj Kadam

Copy Editors
Insiya Morbiwala
Sayanee Mukherjee
Aditya Nair

Project Coordinator
Sageer Parkar

Proofreaders
Simran Bhogal
Ameesha Green

Indexers
Rekha Nair
Tejal Soni

Graphics
Ronak Dhruv

Production Coordinators
Kyle Albuquerque
Saiprasad Kadam
Conidon Miranda

Cover Work
Kyle Albuquerque

About the Author

Basit A. Masood-Al-Farooq is an internationally known Lead SQL DBA, trainer, and technical author with twelve years' experience of the Microsoft technology stack. He is an accomplished development and production SQL Server DBA with a proven record of delivering major projects on time and within budget. He is an expert at evaluating the clients' needs against the capabilities of the SQL Server product set, with the objective of minimizing costs and maximizing functions by making innovative use of advance capabilities. Basit has authored numerous SQL Server technical articles on various SQL Server topics for different SQL Server community sites, which include SQLMag.com, MSSQLTips.com, SQLServerCentral.com, SSWUG.org, SQL-Server-Performance.com, and SearchSQLServer.com.

He has also developed and implemented many successful database infrastructures, data warehouses, and business intelligence projects. He holds a Master's degree in Computer Science from London Metropolitan University and industry-standard certifications from Microsoft, Sun, Cisco, Brainbench, ProSoft, and APM, which include MCITP Database Administrator 2008, MCITP Database Administrator 2005, MCDBA SQL Server 2000 and MCTS .NET Framework 2.0 Web Applications. He also has a good understanding of ITIL principles.

He can be reached via Twitter (@BasitAali), his blog (http://basitaalishan.com), or via LinkedIn (http://uk.linkedin.com/in/basitfarooq).

He was a technical reviewer for *SQL Server 2012 Reporting Services Blueprints*, *Marlon Ribunal and Mickey Stuewe, Packt Publishing* and *Reporting with Microsoft SQL Server 2012, James Serra* and *Bill Anton, Packt Publishing*.

Acknowledgments

First and foremost, I would like to praise and thank Allah SWT, the compassionate, the almighty, the most merciful, who has granted me countless blessings, knowledge, and opportunities. Without the will of Allah SWT, none of this would be possible.

I would like to thank my parents for getting me started on my journey, giving me the opportunity for a great education, allowing me to realize my own potential, and giving me the freedom to choose my career path. Thanks Dad (Masood Ahmad Nisar) and Mom (Saeeda Perveen); you both have always supported me and encouraged me in everything I have ever done. You both have worked extremely hard all your life to give me the life I wanted.

I would like to thank my caring, loving, and supportive wife, Aniqa, for all the encouragement and support. Despite the long days, sleepless nights, and long and exhausting marathons of writing, a few words of love and encouragement from you always successfully wipe away all my fatigue. Thank you for supporting me, coping with my hectic work schedule, and taking care of our kids and household activities, and giving me time so that I can pursue and concentrate on this book-writing project. I would also like to thank my two sons, Saifaan and Rayyan, and would like to dedicate this book to them because they always make me smile and understood on those weekend mornings when I was writing this book instead of playing with them. I hope someday you both will read my book and understand why I spent so much time in front of my laptop.

I would also like to thank Packt Publishing for giving me the opportunity to write this book. Last but not least, I would like to thank Neha Nagwekar, the Acquisition Editor; Neil Alexander, the Content Development Editor; Pankaj Kadam, the Technical Editor; and all the technical reviewers, for their help, advice, and constructive comments, because without their feedback this book would not have been possible.

About the Reviewers

Basavaraj Biradar holds a Master's degree in Computer Applications with gold medals from Gulbarga University, India. Besides these, he has a Microsoft Certified Professional certification in SQL Server 2000. Basavaraj has a rich experience of more than 13 years in designing and developing databases for complex, large, online systems. Currently, Basavaraj is working as Senior Technical Lead in a major IT security company.

Basavaraj writes blogs regularly at http://sqlhints.com on SQL Server technologies and his articles are quite popular in the industry. Basavaraj speaks about SQL Server in Microsoft User Group meetings and in his company as well. You may contact Basavaraj through his e-mail ID, basav@sqlhints.com.

Brenner Grudka Lira has been a data analyst and DBA at Neurotech since 2012. He has a Bachelor's degree in Computer Science and a postgraduate degree in Project Management, both from the Catholic University of Pernambuco in Recife, Brazil.

He also has experience in building and modeling data warehouses and has knowledge in SQL Server and MySQL database management. Today, he is dedicated to the study of project management and database tuning.

He has reviewed *Microsoft SQL Server 2012 Integration Services: An Expert Cookbook*, *Reza Rad and Pedro Perfeito*; *Oracle BI Publisher 11g: A Practical Guide to Enterprise Reporting*, *Daniela Bozdoc*; and *Getting Started with SQL Server 2014 Administration*, *Gethyn Ellis*, all by Packt Publishing.

David Loo is a senior software professional with over 25 years' experience in both software development and people management. He is respected for his ability to focus teams on service excellence and for designing and implementing practical process improvements and solutions. He is always on the lookout for ways to contribute his knowledge and experience of software development, team-building, and development best practices.

He has reviewed *Getting Started with SQL Server 2012 Cube Development, Simon Lidberg* and *Getting Started with SQL Server 2014 Administration, Gethyn Ellis,* both by Packt Publishing.

Richard Louie is a Senior Business Intelligence Developer with over 20 years' experience in software development and project management. He has extensive hands-on experience in Oracle and Microsoft SQL for ETL, SSIS, SSRS, SSAS, and VB.Net. Richard is a graduate of the University of California, Irvine in Information and Computer Science, and is ASQ Green Belt Certified.

He has reviewed *Getting Started with SQL Server 2012 Cube Development, Simon Lidberg* and *Getting Started with SQL Server 2014 Administration, Gethyn Ellis,* both by Packt Publishing.

José (Cheo) Redondo is a consultant, educator, mentor, and evangelist of technology databases and a SQL Server MVP in Latin America, specializing in enterprise databases and business intelligence solutions since 1998. Since that time, he has been providing consulting services and specialized education through academic and business-user groups. He gives conferences to the PASS Community (SQLSaturday events) in Latin America and the US in Spanish, and has been leading SQL PASS Venezuela for several years now. You can follow Cheo on Twitter at `@redondoj` or contact him through his blog, El Blog de Cheo Redondo in Spanish (`http://redondoj.wordpress.com/`), or his e-mail, `redondoj@gmail.com`.

www.PacktPub.com

Support files, eBooks, discount offers, and more

You might want to visit www.PacktPub.com for support files and downloads related to your book.

Did you know that Packt offers eBook versions of every book published, with PDF and ePub files available? You can upgrade to the eBook version at www.PacktPub.com and as a print book customer, you are entitled to a discount on the eBook copy. Get in touch with us at service@packtpub.com for more details.

At www.PacktPub.com, you can also read a collection of free technical articles, sign up for a range of free newsletters and receive exclusive discounts and offers on Packt books and eBooks.

http://PacktLib.PacktPub.com

Do you need instant solutions to your IT questions? PacktLib is Packt's online digital book library. Here, you can access, read and search across Packt's entire library of books.

Why subscribe?
- Fully searchable across every book published by Packt
- Copy and paste, print and bookmark content
- On demand and accessible via web browser

Free access for Packt account holders

If you have an account with Packt at www.PacktPub.com, you can use this to access PacktLib today and view nine entirely free books. Simply use your login credentials for immediate access.

Instant updates on new Packt books

Get notified! Find out when new books are published by following @PacktEnterprise on Twitter, or the *Packt Enterprise* Facebook page.

Table of Contents

Preface

Microsoft SQL Server is an enterprise database server that is the cornerstone of modern business applications and is in the center of the business processes of many leading organizations. The latest release of Microsoft SQL Server, SQL Server 2014, has many new features. These new features of SQL Server 2014 let you design, build, and deploy high-performance OLTP applications. Especially, the new in-memory technology of SQL Server 2014 helps you to design and implement high-performance OLTP applications. According to Microsoft, in some situations, implementing the new SQL Server 2014 in-memory technology for existing OLTP applications can improve the performance of these applications by 10 times. This book will provide you with all the skills you need to successfully design, build, and deploy databases using SQL Server 2014. Starting from the beginning, this book gives you an insight into the key stages of the SQL Server database process, provides you with an in-depth knowledge of the SQL Server database architecture, and shares tips to help you design the new database.

By sequentially working through the steps in each chapter, you will gain hands-on experience in designing, creating, and deploying SQL Server databases and objects. You will learn how to use SQL Server 2014 Management Studio and the advanced Transact-SQL queries to retrieve data from the SQL Server database. You will also learn how to add, modify, and delete data stored within a database. You will use Transact-SQL statements to create and manage advanced database objects that include scalar and table-valued functions, views, stored procedures, and triggers. Finally, you will learn about how the SQL Server 2014 relation engine works, how indexes and statistics improve query performance, and the new SQL Server 2014 in-memory technologies.

What this book covers

Chapter 1, Microsoft SQL Server Database Design Principles, explains the database design process and the architecture and working of the SQL Server 2014 Storage Engine. This chapter covers the database development life cycle in detail, including the normalization and denormalization process, benefits of choosing appropriate data types, and the functioning of the SQL Server 2014 Storage Engine.

Chapter 2, Understanding DDL and DCL Statements in SQL Server, introduces the reader to the SQL Server 2014 Transact-SQL language elements and SQL Server 2014 Management Studio (SSMS 2014). This chapter explains Transact-SQL DDL, DCL, and DML language elements in detail, and how you can use them to create, manage, and secure SQL Server 2014 databases, schemas, and tables. This chapter also shows you how you can use SQL Server Management Studio to create and manage SQL Server 2014 databases, schemas, and tables. Finally, this chapter covers the purpose of SQL Server 2014 system databases and highlights the advantages and disadvantages of database recovery models.

Chapter 3, Data Retrieval Using Transact-SQL Statements, demonstrates how to query data from tables, how to write multiple table queries, and how to group, organize, and pivot result set data. This chapter explores the basic form of the SELECT statement and how it can be used to query data from tables. This chapter also highlights the different categories of built-in T-SQL functions and how you can use them in your SELECT statements. This chapter also explains different techniques that you can use to combine data from multiple tables, how to organize the data, and how to generate the summary data by grouping or pivoting it. Finally, this chapter covers the purpose of the CTE and SQL Server 2014 windowing functions and how to use them to quickly solve complex analytical tasks.

Chapter 4, Data Modification with SQL Server Transact-SQL Statements, illustrates how to add, modify, and delete data in tables using Transact-SQL DML statements. This chapter covers how to add data to a table using the INSERT statement, how to delete the data using the DELETE statement, and how to update existing data using the UPDATE statement. This chapter also covers the SELECT…INTO, MERGE, and TRUNCATE TABLE statements, and it highlights the key new enhancements of these statements in SQL Server 2014.

Chapter 5, Understanding Advanced Database Programming Objects and Error Handling, covers reusable programming objects that includes views, stored procedures (normal and natively compiled), functions and triggers (based on either DDL or DML), SQL Server 2014 control-of-flow statements, and structured error handling blocks. This chapter shows you how you can declare and use variables and how you can use control-of-flow statements to control your program execution. Next, it explains the purpose of views, stored procedures, user-defined functions, and triggers, and highlights the guidelines and restrictions to design each of these programmable objects. This chapter also illustrates how to handle errors that occur within Transact-SQL batches and programmable objects using the TRY...CATCH construct.

Chapter 6, Performance Basics, explains performance-related features of SQL Server 2014. This chapter first explains the architecture of the SQL Server Relational Engine. Then, it introduces the architecture of the SQL Server 2014 in-memory technology. Next, it covers all SQL Server 2014 index types and how they can be used to achieve optimal query performance while reducing the overall response time. Then, it explores the architectural differences of B-tree, Bw-tree, and xVelocity columnstore indexes. Finally, it explains core performance topics such as SQL Server query optimization statistics, SQL Server transactions and locks, and tools that come with SQL Server 2014 Database Engine, which you can use to monitor and troubleshoot its Database Engine performance.

What you need for this book

The following are the software prerequisites to run the samples in the book:

- Windows 7.0 SP1 or later
- SQL Server 2014 Developer edition
- SQL Server Management Studio
- AdventureWorks2012 sample database, which is available for download from the CodePlex site at `http://msftdbprodsamples.codeplex.com/downloads/get/478214`

Who this book is for

If you want to learn how to design, implement, and deliver successful database solutions with SQL Server 2014, this is the book for you.

Conventions

In this book, you will find a number of styles of text that distinguish between different kinds of information. Here are some examples of these styles, and an explanation of their meaning.

Code words in text, database table names, folder names, filenames, file extensions, pathnames, dummy URLs, user input, and Twitter handles are shown as follows: "Each row in the `Customer` table represents an individual customer."

A block of code is set as follows:

```
[default]
DECLARE @Table2 TABLE (
COL1 [int],
COL2 [varchar](30),
COL3 [datetime],
   INDEX [ixc_col3] CLUSTERED (col3)
     WITH (FILLFACTOR=80),
   INDEX [ixnc_col1_col2] NONCLUSTERED (col1, col2)
     WITH (FILLFACTOR=80)
);
```

New terms and **important words** are shown in bold. Words that you see on the screen, in menus or dialog boxes for example, appear in the text like this: "Right-click on **User-Defined Data Types** and choose **New User-Defined Data Type**."

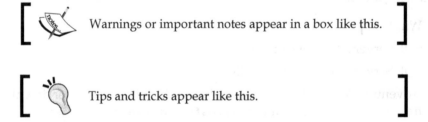

> Warnings or important notes appear in a box like this.

> Tips and tricks appear like this.

Reader feedback

Feedback from our readers is always welcome. Let us know what you think about this book—what you liked or may have disliked. Reader feedback is important for us to develop titles that you really get the most out of.

To send us general feedback, simply send an e-mail to feedback@packtpub.com, and mention the book title via the subject of your message.

If there is a topic that you have expertise in and you are interested in either writing or contributing to a book, see our author guide on www.packtpub.com/authors.

Customer support

Now that you are the proud owner of a Packt book, we have a number of things to help you to get the most from your purchase.

Downloading the example code

You can download the example code files for all Packt books you have purchased from your account at http://www.packtpub.com. If you purchased this book elsewhere, you can visit http://www.packtpub.com/support and register to have the files e-mailed directly to you.

Errata

Although we have taken every care to ensure the accuracy of our content, mistakes do happen. If you find a mistake in one of our books—maybe a mistake in the text or the code—we would be grateful if you would report this to us. By doing so, you can save other readers from frustration and help us improve subsequent versions of this book. If you find any errata, please report them by visiting http://www.packtpub.com/submit-errata, selecting your book, clicking on the **errata submission form** link, and entering the details of your errata. Once your errata are verified, your submission will be accepted and the errata will be uploaded on our website, or added to any list of existing errata, under the Errata section of that title. Any existing errata can be viewed by selecting your title from http://www.packtpub.com/support.

Piracy

Piracy of copyright material on the Internet is an ongoing problem across all media. At Packt, we take the protection of our copyright and licenses very seriously. If you come across any illegal copies of our works, in any form, on the Internet, please provide us with the location address or website name immediately so that we can pursue a remedy.

Please contact us at copyright@packtpub.com with a link to the suspected pirated material.

We appreciate your help in protecting our authors, and our ability to bring you valuable content.

Questions

You can contact us at questions@packtpub.com if you are having a problem with any aspect of the book, and we will do our best to address it.

1
Microsoft SQL Server Database Design Principles

Database design is one of the most important tasks in the **Systems Development Life Cycle (SDLC)**, also referred to as **Application Development Life Cycle (ADLC)**. That's because databases are essential for all businesses, and good design is crucial to any business-critical, high-performance application. Poor database design results in wasted time during the development process and often leads to unusual databases that are unfit for use.

We'll be covering the following topics in this chapter:

- The database design process and considerations
- The table design process, which includes identifying entities and attributes, creating a relationship between entities, and ensuring data integrity
- The basics of data normalization
- The SQL Server database architecture
- The importance of choosing the appropriate data type

Database design

The database design process consists of a number of steps. The general aim of a database design process is to develop an efficient, high-quality database that meets the needs and demands of the application and business stakeholders. Once you have a solid design, you can build the database quickly. In most organizations, database architects and **database administrators (DBAs)** are responsible for designing a database. Their responsibility is to understand the business and operational requirements of an organization, model the database based on these requirements, and establish who will use the database and how. They simply take the lead on the database design project and are responsible for the management and control of the overall database design process.

The database design process can usually be broken down into six phases, as follows:

- The requirement collection and analysis phase
- The conceptual design phase
- The logical design phase
- The physical design phase
- The implementation and loading phase
- The testing and evaluation phase

These phases of design do not have clear boundaries and are not strictly linear. In addition, the design phases might overlap, and you will often find that due to real-world limitations, you might have to revisit a previous design phase and rework some of your initial assumptions.

The requirement collection and analysis phase

In this phase, you interview the prospective users, gather their requirements, and discuss their expectations from the new database application. Your objective in this phase is to gather as much information as possible from potential users and then document these requirements. This phase results in a concise set of user and functional requirements, which should be detailed and complete. Functional requirements typically include user operations that need to be applied to the database, information flow, type of operation, frequency of transactions, and data updates. You can document functional requirements using diagrams, such as sequence diagrams, **data flow diagrams (DFDs)**, scenarios, and so on.

Moreover, you can also conduct an analysis of the current operating environment—whether it's manual, a file processing system, or an old DBMS system—and interact with users extensively to analyze the nature of the business to be supported; you can also justify the need for data and databases. The requirement collection and analysis phase can take a significant amount of time; however, it plays a vital role in the success of the new database application. The outcome of this phase is the document that contains the user's specifications, which is then used as the basis for the design of the new database application.

The conceptual design phase

Your goal during the conceptual design phase is to develop the conceptual schema of the database, which is then used to ensure that all user requirements are met and do not conflict. In this step, you need to select the appropriate data model and then translate the requirements that arise from the preceding phase into the conceptual database schema by applying the concepts of the chosen data model, which does not depend on RDBMS. The most general data model used in this phase is the **entity-relationship (ER)** model, which is usually used to represent the conceptual database design. The conceptual schema includes a concise description of the user's data requirements, including a detailed description of the entity types, relationships, and constraints.

The conceptual design phase does not include the implementation details. Thus, end users can easily understand them, and they can be used as a communication tool. During this phase, you are not concerned with how the solution will be implemented. In the conceptual design phase, you only make general design decisions that may or may not hold when you start looking at the technologies and project budget available. The information you gather during the conceptual design phase is critical to the success of your database design.

The logical design phase

During the logical design phase, you map the high-level, conceptual, entity-relationship data model into selected RDBMS constructs. The data model that is chosen will represent the company and its operations. From there, a framework of how to provide a solution based on the data model will be developed. In this phase, you also determine the best way to represent the data, the services required by the solution, and how to implement these services. The data model of a logical design will be a more detailed framework than the one developed during the conceptual design phase. This phase provides specific guidelines, which you can use to create the physical database design.

You do little, if any, physical implementation work at this point, although you may want to do a limited prototyping to see whether the solution meets user expectations.

The physical design phase

During the physical design phase, you make decisions about the database environment (database server), application development environment, database file organization, physical database objects, and so on. The physical design phase is a very technical stage in the database design process. The result of this phase will be a physical design specification that will be used to build and deploy your database solution.

The implementation and loading phase

During this phase, you implement the proposed database solution. The phase includes activities such as the creation of the database, the compilation and execution of **Data Definition Language** (DDL) statements to create the database schema and database files, the manual or automatic loading of the data into a new database system from a previous system, and finally, the configuration of the database and application security.

The testing and evaluation phase

In this phase, you perform the testing of your database solution to tune it for performance, integrity, concurrent access, and security restrictions. Typically, this is done in parallel with the application programming phase. If the test fails, you take several actions such as adjusting the performance based on a reference manual, modifying the physical design, modifying the logical design, and upgrading or changing the SQL Server software and database server hardware.

The database design life cycle recap

The following diagram briefly illustrates the database design process:

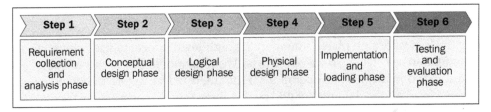

Table design

As mentioned earlier, you complete the table and data design activities during the conceptual and logical design phases of the database design. During the conceptual design phase, you identify specific data needs and determine how to present the data in the database solution, which is based on the information you collected in the requirement gathering phase. You then use the information from the conceptual design phase in the logical design phase to design and organize your data structure. In the logical design phase, you also identify the requirements for database objects to store and organize the data.

Often, one of the most time-consuming and important tasks in the physical design phase is the table design. During the physical design phase, you identify the following:

- Entities and attributes
- Relationships between entities

Tables

You use tables to store and organize data in the database. A table contains columns and rows. For example, the following is an example of how a Customer table might look. Each row in the Customer table represents an individual customer. The column contains information that describes the data for the individual customer. Each column has a data type, which identifies a format in which the data is stored in that column. Some data types can have a fixed length, which means that the size does not depend on the data stored in it. You also have data types with variable lengths, which means their length changes to fit the data they possess.

Entities

Entities are business objects that your database contains, and they are used to logically separate the data in the database. An entities list, which you need to create, is used to determine the tables as part of the physical design phase. You create a separate table in the database for each entity (such as customers, employees, orders, and the payroll). Entities are characterized by attributes. For example, you declare each individual attribute of an entity (such as an individual customer, an individual order, an individual employee, or an individual payroll record) as a row in the table.

Attributes

An attribute is a property of an entity. For example, the employee entity has attributes such as the employee ID, first name, last name, birthday, social security number, address, country, and so on. Some attributes are unique values. For example, each customer in a `Customer` table has a unique customer number. Attributes are used to organize specific data within the entity.

Relationships

Relationships identify associations between the data stored in different tables. Entities relate to other entities in a variety of ways. Table relationships come in several forms, listed as follows:

- A one-to-one relationship
- A one-to-many relationship
- A many-to-many relationship

A one-to-one relationship

A one-to-one relationship represents a relationship between entities in which one occurrence of data is related to one and only one occurrence of data in the related entity. For example, every employee should have a payroll record, but only one payroll record. Have a look at the following diagram to get a better understanding of one-to-one relationships:

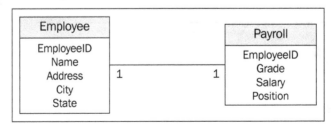

A one-to-many relationship

A one-to-many relationship seems to be the most common relationship that exists in relational databases. In the one-to-many relationship, each occurrence of data in one entity is related to zero or more occurrences of data in a second entity. For example, each department in a `Department` table can have one or more employees in the `Employee` table. The following diagram will give you a better understanding of one-to-many relationships:

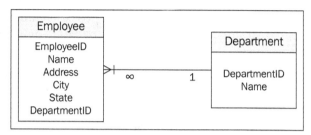

A many-to-many relationship

In a many-to-many relationship, each occurrence of data in one entity is related to zero or more occurrences of data in a second entity, and at the same time, each occurrence of the second entity is related to zero or more occurrences of data in the first entity. For example, one instructor teaches many classes, and one class is taught by many instructors, as shown in the following diagram:

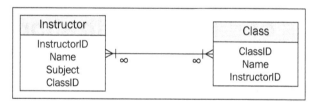

A many-to-many relationship often causes problems in practical examples of normalized databases, and therefore, it is common to simply break many-to-many relationships in to a series of one-to-many relationships.

Data integrity

Data integrity ensures that the data within the database is reliable and adheres to business rules. Data integrity falls into the following categories:

- **Domain integrity**: This ensures that the values of the specified columns are legal, which means domain integrity ensures that the value meets a specified format and value criteria. You can enforce domain integrity by restricting the type of data stored within columns (through data types), the format (through CHECK constraints and rules), or the range of possible values (through FOREIGN KEY constraints, CHECK constraints, DEFAULT definitions, NOT NULL definitions, and rules).

- **Entity integrity**: This ensures that every row in the table is uniquely identified by requiring a unique value in one or more key columns of the table. You can enforce entity integrity through indexes, UNIQUE KEY constraints, PRIMARY KEY constraints, or IDENTITY properties.

- **Referential integrity**: This ensures that the data is consistent between related tables. You can enforce referential integrity through PRIMARY KEY constraints and FOREIGN KEY constraints.

- **User-defined integrity**: This ensures that the values stored in the database remain consistent with established business policies. You can maintain user-defined integrity through business rules and enforce user-integrity through stored procedures and triggers.

The basics of data normalization

Normalization is the process of reducing or completely eliminating the occurrence of redundant data in the database. Normalization refers to the process of designing relational database tables from the ER model. It is a part of the logical design process and is a requirement for **online transaction processing (OLTP)** databases. This is important because it eliminates (or reduces as much as possible) redundant data. During the normalization process, you usually split large tables with many columns into one or more smaller tables with a smaller number of columns. The main advantage of normalization is to promote data consistency between tables and data accuracy by reducing the redundant information that is stored. In essence, data only needs to be changed in one place if an occurrence of the data is stored only once.

The disadvantage of normalization is that it produces many tables with a relatively small number of columns. These columns have to then be joined together in order for the data to be retrieved. Normalization could affect the performance of a database drastically. In fact, the more the database is normalized, the more the performance will suffer.

The normal forms

Traditional definitions of normalization refer to the process of modifying database tables to adhere to accepted normal forms. Normal forms are the rules of normalization. They are a way to measure the levels or depth that a database is normalized to. There are five different normal forms; however, most database solutions are implemented with the **third normal form** (**3NF**). Both the **forth normal form** (**4NF**) and the **fifth normal form** (**5NF**) are rarely used and, hence, are not discussed in this chapter. Each normal form builds from the previous. For example, the **second normal form** (**2NF**) cannot begin before the **first normal form** (**1NF**) is completed.

 A detailed discussion of all of the normal forms is outside the scope of this book. For help with this, refer to the Wikipedia article at `http://en.wikipedia.org/wiki/Database_normalization`.

The first normal form (1NF)

In 1NF, you divide the base data into logical units called entities or tables. When you design each entity or table, you assign the primary key to it, which uniquely identifies each record inside the table. You create a separate table for each set of related attributes. There can be only one value for each attribute or column heading. The 1NF eliminates the repetition of groups by putting each one in a separate table and connecting them with a one-to-many relationship.

The second normal form (2NF)

The objective of 2NF is to avoid the duplication of data between tables. In 2NF, you take data that is partly dependent on the primary key and enter it into another table. The entity is in 2NF when it meets all of the requirements of 1NF and has no composite primary key. In 2NF, you cannot subdivide the primary key into separate logical entities. You can, however, eliminate functional dependencies on partial keys by putting those fields in a separate table from the ones that are dependent on the whole key.

The third normal form (3NF)

The 3NF objective is used to remove the data in a table that is not dependant on the primary key. In 3NF, no non-key column can depend on another non-key column, so all of the data applies specifically to the table entity. The entity is in 3NF when it meets all of the requirements of 1NF and 2NF and there is no transitive functional dependency.

Denormalization

Denormalization is the reverse of the normalization process, where you combine smaller tables that contain related attributes. Applications such as **online analytical processing (OLAP)** applications are good candidates for denormalized data. This is because all of the necessary data is in one place, and SQL Server does not require to combine data when queried.

The SQL Server database architecture

SQL Server maps the database over a set of operating system files that store the database objects. Physically, a SQL Server database is a set of two or more operating system files. Each database file has two names:

- **A logical filename**: This is the name you reference in Transact-SQL statements
- **A physical filename**: This is the name that you can view in the operating system directory tree

SQL Server database files can be stored on either a FAT or an NTFS filesystem. You can create three types of SQL Server database files, listed as follows:

- **Primary data file**: This is the initial default file that contains the configuration information for the database, pointers to the other files in the database, and all of the database objects. Every database has one primary data file. The preferred filename extension for a primary data file is .mdf. Although you can store user objects within the main data file, but it is not recommended.

- **Secondary data file**: Secondary data files are optional and used to hold user database objects. You can create one or more secondary files within the database to hold the user database objects. The recommend filename extension for a secondary data file is .ndf. Secondary data files can be spread across multiple disks and are useful as the database's additional storage area.

- **Transaction log file**: This is the log file for the database that holds information about all database modification events. The information in the transaction log file is used to recover the database. A database can have one or more transaction log files. Multiple transaction log files do not improve database performance as the SQL Server database engine writes log information sequentially. The recommended filename extension for transaction logs is `.ldf`.

Pages

SQL Server uses pages as a basic unit of data storage. The disk space allocated to a data file (`.mdf` or `.ndf`) in a database is logically divided into pages that are numbered contiguously from 0 to *n*. SQL Server performs disk I/O operations at a page level, which means that the SQL Server database engine reads or writes the whole data page during the **Data Manipulation Language** (**DML**) operation.

In SQL Server, the page is an 8 KB block of contiguous disk space. SQL Server can store 128 pages per megabyte of allocated storage space. Each page starts with 96 bytes of header information about the page. If the rows are small, multiple rows can be stored on a page, as shown in the following diagram:

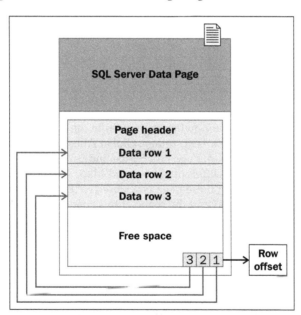

The rows of a SQL Server table cannot span multiple pages of data. That is why the rows are limited to a maximum of 8,060 bytes of data. However, there is an exception to this rule for data types that are used to store large blocks of text. The data for such data types is stored separately from the pages of the small row data. For example, if you have a row that exceeds 8,060 bytes, which includes a column that contains large blocks of text, SQL Server dynamically moves this text to a separate text/image page, as shown in the following diagram:

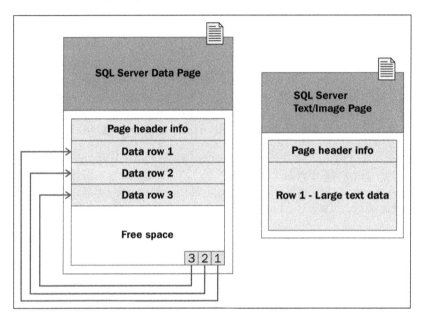

 SQL Server uses the following page types in the data files of a SQL Server database: Data, Index, Text/Image, Global Allocation Map, Shared Global Allocation Map, Page Free Space, Index Allocation Map, Bulk Changed Map, and Differential Changed Map. A detailed discussion about the contents of these page types used in the data files of a SQL Server database is beyond the scope of this chapter. For help with this, refer to the *Understanding Pages and Extents* article at http://technet.microsoft.com/en-US/library/ms190969(v=sql.120).aspx.

Extents

An extent is eight contiguous pages (64 KB) of disk storage. SQL Server can store 16 extents per megabyte of allocated storage space. A small table can share extents with other database objects to make better use of available space, with the limitation of eight objects per extent. Each page in an extent can be owned by different user objects as shown in the following diagram:

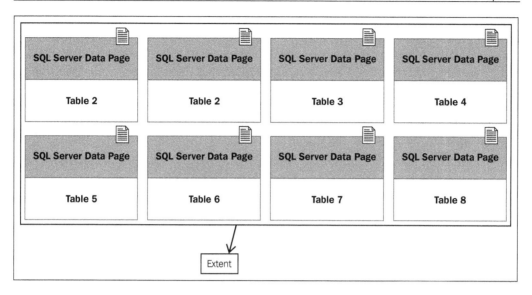

The transaction log file architecture

SQL Server database transaction log files contain the information that is needed to recover the SQL Server database if a system failure occurs. A database can have one or more transaction log files. SQL Server records each DML operation performed against the database in the transaction log file. When a system failure occurs, SQL Server enters into the automatic recovery mode on startup, and it uses the information in the transaction log to recover the database. The automatic recovery process rolls committed transactions forward (which means that it makes changes to the database) and reverts any uncommitted transactions post system failure.

SQL Server divides the physical transaction log file into smaller segments called **Virtual Log Files** (**VLFs**). The virtual log file only contains a log record for active transactions. SQL Server truncates the virtual log file once it is no longer contains active transactions. The virtual log file has no fixed size, and there is no fixed number of virtual log files per physical transaction log file. You cannot configure the size and number of virtual log files; the SQL Server database engine dynamically manages the size and number of the virtual log files each time you create or extend the physical transaction log file.

SQL Server tries to keep the number of virtual log files to a minimum; however, you will end up with too many virtual log files if you incorrectly size the physical transaction log file or set it to grow in small increments. This is because whenever the physical transaction log file grows, the SQL Server database engine adds more virtual log files to the physical transaction log file. Having too many virtual log files can significantly impair the performance of the database. Therefore, you need to periodically monitor the physical transaction log file to check for a high number of virtual log files. You can run DBCC LOGINFO to check the number of the virtual log files in the database. The following is the syntax of this command:

```
USE [YourDatabaseName];
DBCC LOGINFO;
```

You can also use DBCC SQLPREF to view the amount of space available in the transaction log file.

The operation and workings of a transaction log

The following diagram illustrates the workings of the transaction log during the data manipulation language operation:

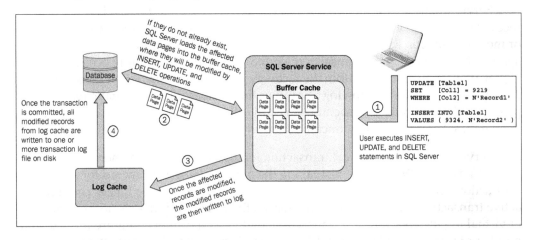

The SQL Server database transaction log acts as a write-ahead log (as SQL Sever writes to the log before writing to the disk) for modifications to the database, which means that the modification of the data is not written to disk until a checkpoint occurs in the database. For example, as illustrated in the previous diagram, when you execute an INSERT, UPDATE, or DELETE statement, the SQL Server database engine first checks the buffer cache for the affected data pages. If the affected data pages are not in the buffer cache, the SQL Server database engine loads these affected data pages into a buffer cache.

The SQL Server database engine then logs the operation in the log cache, which is another designated area in memory. When the transaction is committed, the modifications associated with the transaction are written from the log cache to the transaction log file on disk. Completed transactions are written to the database periodically by the checkpoint process.

Filegroups

In SQL Server databases, you can group the secondary data files logically for administrative purposes. This administrative grouping of data files is called filegroups. By default, the SQL Server databases are created with one filegroup, also known as the default filegroup (or primary filegroup) for the database. The primary database is a member of the default filegroup. You can add secondary database files to the default filegroup; however, this is not recommended. It is recommended that you create separate filegroups for your secondary data files. This is known as a secondary filegroup (or user-defined filegroup). The SQL Server database engine allows you to create one or more filegroups, which can contain one or more secondary data files. Transaction log files do not belong to any filegroup. You can query the sys.filegroups system catalog to list all of the information about filegroups created within the SQL Server database.

The main advantage of filegroups is that they can be backed up or restored separately, or they can be brought online or taken offline separately.

 We will learn about creating a database and filegroups in the next chapter.

The importance of choosing the appropriate data type

A data type determines the type of data that can be stored in a database table column. When you create a table, you must decide on the data type to be used for the column definitions. You can also use data types to define variables and store procedure input and output parameters. You must select a data type for each column or variable appropriate for the data stored in that column or variable. In addition, you must consider storage requirements and choose data types that allow for efficient storage. For example, you should always use tinyint instead of smallint, int, or bigint if you want to store whole positive integers between 0 and 255. This is because tinyint is a fixed 1-byte field, whereas smallint is 2 bytes, int is 4 bytes, and bigint is a fixed 8-byte field.

Choosing the right data types for your tables, stored procedures, and variables not only improves performance by ensuring a correct execution plan, but it also improves data integrity by ensuring that the correct data is stored within a database. For example, if you use a `datetime` data type for a column of dates, then only valid dates will be stored in this column. However, if you use a character or numeric data type for the column, then eventually, someone will be able to store any type of character or numeric data value in the column that does not represent a date.

SQL Server 2014 supports three basic data types: system data types defined by SQL Server, alias data types based on system data types, and .NET Framework **common language runtime (CLR) user-defined data types (UDT)**.

SQL Server 2014 system data types

SQL Server defines a wide variety of system data types that are designed to meet most of your data storage requirements. The system data types are organized into the following categories:

- Exact numeric data types include `bigint`, `int`, `smallint`, `tinyint`, `bit`, `numeric`, `money`, and `smallmoney`
- Approximate numeric data types include `float` and `real`
- Character string data types include `char`, `varchar`, and `text`
- Unicode character string data types include `nchar`, `nvarchar`, and `ntext`
- Date and time data types include `date`, `time`, `smalldatetime`, `datetime`, `datetime2`, and `datetimeoffset`
- Binary string data types include: `binary`, `varbinary`, and `image`
- Other data types include `cursor`, `timestamp`, `hierarchyid`, `uniqueidentifier`, `sql_variant`, `xml`, `table`, and spatial types (`geometry` and `geography`)

Out of these data types, the following data types are not supported in memory-optimized tables and natively compiled stored procedures: `datetimeoffset`, `geography`, `geometry`, `hierarchyid`, `rowversion`, `sql_variant`, UDT, `xml`, `varchar(max)`, `nvarchar(max)`, `image`, `xml`, `text`, and `ntext`. This is because the size of the memory-optimized tables is limited to 8,060 bytes, and they do not support off-row or **large object (LOB)** storage.

For more information on the data types supported in memory-optimized tables and natively compiled stored procedures, refer to the *Supported Data Types* article at `http://msdn.microsoft.com/en-us/library/dn133179(v=sql.120).aspx`.

Alias data types

In SQL Server, you can create alias data types, also known as user-defined data types. The purpose of the alias data types is to create a custom data type to help ensure data consistency. The alias data types are based on system data types. You can either use SQL Server 2014 Management Studio or the CREATE TYPE and DROP TYPE Transact-SQL DDL statements to create and drop alias data types.

Creating and dropping alias data types with SSMS 2014

Perform the following steps to create alias data types:

1. Launch SQL Server 2014 Management Studio.

2. In **Object Explorer**, expand the Databases folder, then the database for which you want to see user-defined types, then Programmability, and then Types.

3. Right-click on **User-Defined Data Types** and choose **New User-Defined Data Type**.

4. Enter the information about the data type you want to create.

To drop the alias data type, right-click on the data type and choose **Delete**.

Creating and dropping alias data types using the Transact-SQL DDL statement

In this section, we will use the CREATE TYPE and DROP TYPE Transact-SQL DDL statements to create and drop alias data types.

Creating an alias data type using CREATE TYPE

The following is the basic syntax for the CREATE TYPE Transact-SQL DDL statement:

```
CREATE TYPE [schema.]name
FROM base_type[(precision [, scale])] [NULL | NOT NULL] [;]
```

In the following example, T-SQL code creates the alias data type called account_type to hold the six-character book type:

```
CREATE TYPE dbo.account_type
FROM char(6) NOT NULL;
```

Dropping an alias data type using DROP TYPE

The following is the basic syntax for the DROP TYPE Transact-SQL DDL statement:

```
DROP TYPE [schema.]name [;]
```

The following example T-SQL code drops the alias data type called account_type:

```
DROP TYPE dbo.account_type
```

CLR user-defined types

CLR user-defined types are data types based on CLR assemblies. A detailed discussion on CLR data types is outside the scope of this chapter. For help with this, refer to the *CLR User-Defined Types* article at http://msdn.microsoft.com/en-us/library/ms131120(v=sql.120).aspx.

Summary

Designing a new database is very similar to designing anything else, such as a building, a car, a road, a bridge through the city, or a book like this one. In this chapter, we learned about the key stages to design a new database. Next, we talked about the normal form, the process of normalizing and denormalizing data, entities, attributes, relationships, and data integrity. Then, we learned about the architecture of SQL Server databases and got an understanding of how SQL Server uses the transaction log when you execute INSERT, UPDATE, or DELETE statements in SQL Server. Finally, we learned about why it is important to choose appropriate data types for your databases.

2
Understanding DDL and DCL Statements in SQL Server

Once you have completed the physical design phase of the database design process, the next step is to implement your proposed database solution.

The **Structured Query Language (SQL)** of Microsoft SQL Server is called **Transact-SQL (T-SQL)**. The Transact-SQL statements have three categories: **Data Definition Language (DDL)** statements, **Data Control Language (DCL)** statements, and **Data Manipulation Language (DML)** statements that can be used to create, modify, and query SQL Server databases and tables.

In this chapter, we'll be covering the following topics:

- Understanding DDL, DCL, and DML language elements
- Understanding the purpose of SQL Server 2014 system databases
- Exploring database recovery models
- Creating and modifying databases
- Creating and modifying database schemas
- Creating and modifying tables
- Grating, revoking, and denying permissions to securables

Understanding the DDL, DCL, and DML language elements

As mentioned earlier, the Transact-SQL statements have three categories: DDL statements, DCL statements, and DML statements. Each of the commands in these categories include keywords and parameters that can be used to create, modify, and query SQL Server 2014 databases and tables. Let's have a quick look at the keywords and the purpose of each T-SQL statement type in the following sections.

Data Definition Language (DDL) statements

The T-SQL DDL statements include keywords that you can use to create databases and database objects, modify databases and database objects, and remove databases and database objects. The DDL statements consist of the following keywords: CREATE, ALTER, and DROP. Using these DDL keywords, you can create and modify the structure of your databases and create and modify all kinds of database objects (tables, schemas, indexes, stored procedures, functions, views, triggers, login accounts, database users, server and database roles, credentials, extended events, event notifications, and service broker objects).

To execute DDL statements, you must have the appropriate permissions to SQL Server and database. By default, members of the sysadmin fixed server role and the db_owner fixed database role have permissions to execute DDL statements.

Data Manipulation Language (DML) statements

We use DML statements to insert, update, delete, and query data that is stored in SQL Server database tables. The DML statements consist of the following commands: SELECT, INSERT, BULK INSERT, UPDATE, MERGE, and DELETE.

To execute DML statements, you must have the appropriate permissions in the database. By default, members of the sysadmin fixed server role and the db_owner and db_writer fixed database roles have the permissions to execute DML statements.

Data Control Language (DCL) statements

DCL statements enable you to grant, deny, and revoke permissions on databases and database objects. The DCL statements include the standard GRANT and REVOKE keywords, as well as the T-SQL DENY statement.

To execute DCL statements, you must have the appropriate permissions for the database. By default, members of the sysadmin and securityadmin fixed server roles and the db_owner and db_securityadmin fixed database roles have the permissions to execute DCL statements.

In this chapter, we will use the DDL commands to create, modify, and delete databases and tables, and DCL commands to grant, deny, and revoke permissions on databases and tables.

We will discuss the DML commands in the next two chapters.

Understanding the purpose of SQL Server 2014 system databases

Before you start creating databases on a SQL Server 2014 instance, you should have a good understanding of the system databases that are installed by default when a SQL Server 2014 instance is created. Each SQL Server 2014 system database has a specific purpose and is required to run SQL Server. So, having a good understanding of the SQL Server system databases is useful when you are troubleshooting SQL Server issues.

SQL Server 2014 system databases

By default, when you install a SQL Server 2014 instance, the SQL Server 2014 setup program creates the following five system databases: master, model, msdb, tempdb, and resource. Apart from these system databases, there is another system database called distribution that does not exist until you configure replication on the SQL Server instance.

The master database

The master database, as its name implies, is the most important database in a SQL Server 2014 instance. In fact, it is the heart of a SQL Server 2014 instance because, without it, SQL Server will not start. The master database contains the following system-level configuration information:

- Information on how a SQL Server 2014 instance is initialized
- The names, locations, and other information about the databases hosted within the instance of SQL Server 2014

- All settings for logins, and the roles the logins are members of
- Information about fixed and user-defined server roles
- Other SQL Server instance-level security settings (such as certificates, keys, and so on)
- AlwaysOn and database mirroring configuration information
- Resource Governor configuration information
- Information about how linked servers are configured
- Configuration information of all SQL Server 2014 instance endpoints
- Other system-level configuration settings (such as system errors and warnings, assemblies, available system languages, and so on)

The model database

The model database is used as a template for creating a new database. In other words, every new database is modeled on a model database. Any modifications (such as a minimum size, default objects, predefined database users, and so on) made in the model database are automatically applied to the databases that are created afterwards.

The msdb database

The msdb database is another critical database within a SQL Server 2014 instance, as it acts as a backend database for the Microsoft SQL Server Agent service. For example, the msdb database contains job scheduling and job history information.

The msdb database also stores information about many other features of SQL Server. These SQL Server features are alerts, SSIS packages, database mail, the database backup and restore feature, maintenance plans, log shipping, **change data capture (CDC)**, and service broker.

The tempdb database

The tempdb database is a temporary shared workspace for temporary objects that are created by internal processes of the SQL Server Database Engine instance and temporary objects that are created by users or applications' processes. These temporary objects include local and global temporary tables, stored procedures, table variables, and cursors. In addition to temporary objects, tempdb acts as a version store for read-committed and snapshot isolation transactions. Furthermore, tempdb stores online index operations, intermediate query results, database consistency checks, bulk load operations for tables with triggers, and AFTER triggers. The tempdb database is automatically recreated every time SQL Server is restarted.

The resource database

The `resource` database is a hidden read-only database that acts as a physical store for SQL Server instance system objects such as system tables, metadata, and system-stored procedures. These system objects are referenced logically by other databases.

The `resource` database does not contain any user data, information about your SQL Server instance, or databases hosted on the SQL Server instance. You should not move or rename the `resource` database because SQL Server will not start if you do so.

The distribution database

The `distribution` database stores all metadata for replication. The `distribution` database is created only on replication distributors. The `distribution` database does not exist until you configure replication on the SQL Server instance.

An overview of database recovery models

The recovery model determines how the transactions are logged, whether the backups of transaction logs are allowed, and the type of restore options available to recover the database. The SQL Server 2014 database can be configured to one of three recovery models, which are explained in the following sections.

The simple recovery model

When you use the simple recovery model, SQL Server logs a minimal amount of transactions in the transaction log file, and the transaction log is truncated as soon as transactions are committed. Simple recovery does not allow backups of transaction log files; therefore, databases with a simple recovery model are vulnerable to data loss because you cannot restore the databases to a specific point in time.

The bulk-logged recovery model

With the bulk-logged recovery model, bulk operations are minimally logged in the transaction log file, reducing the overall size of the transaction log file. All other operations are fully logged in the transaction log file. The backups of transaction log files are allowed in a bulk-logged recovery model. Therefore, in most situations, you can restore the databases to a specific point in time using the bulk-logged recovery model.

Full recovery

With a full recovery model, SQL Server logs all database changes in the transaction log, and the transaction log continues to grow until the backup is performed. The full recovery model supports the greatest number of backup and restore options. Therefore, you can recover to a specific point in time.

Creating and modifying databases

You can use either Transact-SQL DDL statements or SQL Server Management Studio to create and modify databases. In the following subsections, we will discuss these options.

Create, modify, and drop databases with T-SQL DDL statements

In this section, we will cover Transact-SQL DDL statements that are used to create, alter and modify SQL Server databases.

Creating a database with T-SQL DDL statements

We use the CREATE DATABASE statement to create a new database on SQL Server. The general syntax for the CREATE DATABASE command is as follows:

```
CREATE DATABASE database_name
[CONTAINMENT = {NONE | PARTIAL}]
[ON [PRIMARY] [<filespec> [,...n]
[,<filegroup> [,...n]]
[LOG ON <filespec> [,...n]]]
[COLLATE collation_name]
[WITH <option> [,...n]]
[;]
```

The following are the arguments of the CREATE DATABASE command:

- database_name: This is the name of new SQL Server database. The database name must be unique with an instance of SQL Server.

- CONTAINMENT: This is used to specify the containment status of the database. Specify NONE for non-contained databases, and PARTIAL for partially contained databases.

- `ON [PRIMARY]`: This is used to specify the files in the primary filegroup. If this parameter is not specified, the first file in the list becomes the primary file for the database.

- `LOG ON`: This is used to specify the location for the transaction log files.

- `filespec`: The `filespec` arguments are used to control file properties. This option is supported for both the data and transaction log file. The `filespec` parameters include:

  - `Name`: This is the logical name of the database. We use this name in Transact-SQL statements to refer to the file.

  - `FILENAME`: This specifies the operating system name and file path.

> SQL Server 2014 Database Engine enables you to store SQL Server database files as Windows Azure Blobs Storage. This is one of the new features of SQL Server 2014. For more information about this feature, refer to the *SQL Server Data Files in Windows Azure* article at `http://msdn.microsoft.com/en-us/library/dn385720.aspx`.

  - `Size`: This is the initial size of the database file. The value can be specified in KB, MB, GB, or TB.

  - `MAXSIZE`: This is used to specify the maximum size limit for the database file. The value can be specified in KB, MB, GB, TB, or as `UNLIMITED`.

  - `FILEGROWTH`: This is used to specify the automatic growth increments for the database file. The value can be specified in KB, MB, GB, TB, or percentage (%).

- `COLLATE`: This specifies the default collation setting for the database. If not specified, the server default collation is used as the database collation. For more information about the Windows and SQL collation names, refer to the *COLLATE (Transact-SQL)* topic at `http://msdn.microsoft.com/en-gb/library/ms184391(v=sql.120).aspx`.

- `WITH <option>`: This is used to configure the following external excess options:

  - `DEFAULT_FULLTEXT_LANGUAGE`
  - `DEFAULT_LANGUAGE`
  - `DB_CHAINING, TRUSTWORTHY`
  - `NESTED_TRIGGERS`
  - `TWO_DIGIT_YEAR_CUTOFF`
  - `TRANSFORM_NOISE_WORDS`

> A detailed discussion about a database's external excess options
> is beyond the scope of this chapter. For help with this, refer
> to http://technet.microsoft.com/en-us/library/
> ms176061(v=sql.120).aspx.

Example 1 – creating a database based on a model database

The following CREATE DATABASE script creates a CH02_01 database using the default parameters from the model database:

```
USE [master];
GO


CREATE DATABASE [CH02_01];
GO
```

Downloading the example code

You can download the example code files for all Packt books you
have purchased from your account at http://www.packtpub.com.
If you purchased this book elsewhere, you can visit http://www.
packtpub.com/support and register to have the files e-mailed
directly to you.

Example 2 – creating a database that explicitly specifies the database data and the transaction log file's filespecs properties

The following CREATE DATABASE script creates the CH02_02 database by explicitly specifying data and the transaction log file's filespecs properties:

```
USE [master];
GO


CREATE DATABASE CH02_02 ON PRIMARY
(NAME='CH02_02_Data', FILENAME = 'C:\SQLDATA\CH02_02.mdf',
SIZE=10MB, MAXSIZE=20, FILEGROWTH=10%)
    LOG ON
(NAME='CH02_02_log', FILENAME = 'C:\SQLLog\CH02_02_log.ldf',
SIZE=10MB, MAXSIZE=200, FILEGROWTH=20%);
GO
```

Example 3 – creating a database on multiple filegroups

The following CREATE DATABASE script creates the CH02_03 database on the following two filegroups:

- The primary filegroup, which contains CH02_03DAT01 and CH02_02DAT02

- The user-defined filegroup, CH02_FG1, which only contains the database file, that is, CH02_03DAT03

The following code generates the CH02_03 database:

```
USE [master];
GO


CREATE DATABASE [CH02_03]
 CONTAINMENT = NONE
 ON PRIMARY
(NAME = N'CH02_03DAT01 ', FILENAME = N'C:\Program Files\Microsoft
SQL Server\MSSQL12.MSSQLSERVER\MSSQL\DATA\CH02_03DAT01.mdf', SIZE
= 524288KB, FILEGROWTH = 102400KB),
(NAME = N'CH02_03DAT02', FILENAME = N'C:\Program Files\Microsoft
SQL Server\MSSQL12.MSSQLSERVER\MSSQL\DATA\CH02_03DAT02.ndf', SIZE
= 524288KB, FILEGROWTH = 102400KB),
 FILEGROUP [CH02_FG1]
(NAME = N'CH02_03DAT03', FILENAME = N'C:\Program Files\Microsoft
SQL Server\MSSQL12.MSSQLSERVER\MSSQL\DATA\CH02_03DAT03.ndf', SIZE
= 262144KB, FILEGROWTH = 102400KB)
 LOG ON
(NAME = N'CH02_03_log', FILENAME = N'C:\Program Files\Microsoft
SQL Server\MSSQL12.MSSQLSERVER\MSSQL\DATA\CH02_03_log.ldf', SIZE =
262144KB, FILEGROWTH = 102400KB)
GO
```

Modifying a database with T-SQL DDL statements

We use ALTER DATABASE to modify an existing SQL Server database. Some common situations for modifying an existing SQL Server database include:

- Adding or removing filegroups and database files to an existing database

- Adding or removing transaction log files to an existing database

- Manually expanding data and/or transaction log file sizes

- Changing data and/or transaction log file growth settings
- Setting database options
- Changing the database default collation

The following is the basic syntax for the `ALTER DATABASE` statement:

```
ALTER DATABASE database_name
ADD FILE <filespec> [,...n]
[TO FILEGROUP {filegroup_name | DEFAULT}]
| ADD LOG FILE <filespec> [,...n]
| REMOVE FILE logical_filename
| MODIFY FILE filespec
```

The following are the arguments of the `ALTER DATABASE` command:

- `database_name`: This is the name of a new SQL Server database. The database name must be unique with an instance of SQL Server.
- `ADD FILE`: This argument adds a file to the database.
- `TO FILEGROUP`: This will be the name of the filegroup to which the specified file will be added.
- `REMOVE FILE`: This argument removes a file from the database.
- `MODIFY FILE`: This argument specifies the file that should be modified.

Example – adding a secondary data file to an existing database

The following example uses `ALTER DATABASE` to add a secondary data file to the `CH2_03` database user-defined filegroup (`CH02_FG1`):

```
USE [master];
GO
ALTER DATABASE [CH02_03] ADD FILE (NAME = N'CH02_03DAT04',
FILENAME = N'C:\Program Files\Microsoft SQL
Server\MSSQL12.MSSQLSERVER\MSSQL\DATA\CH02_03DAT04.ndf', SIZE =
524288KB, FILEGROWTH = 102400KB) TO FILEGROUP [CH02_FG1];
GO
```

You can also use the SET clause of the ALTER DATABASE statement to change database options. For example, you can run the following command to set the recovery model of the CH02_03 database to FULL:

```
USE [master];
GO


ALTER DATABASE [CH02_03] SET RECOVERY FULL WITH NO_WAIT;
GO
```

Dropping a database with T-SQL DDL statements

When you no longer need a database, you can use the DROP DATABASE statement to delete the database from SQL Server. The following is the basic syntax for DROP DATABASE:

```
DROP DATABASE database_name;
```

For example, you run the following command to drop the CH02_01 database:

```
USE [master];
GO


DROP DATABASE CH02_01;
GO
```

Create, modify, and drop databases with SSMS 2014

You can also use SQL Server 2014 Management Studio to create, modify, and drop SQL Server databases. In this section, we will cover this GUI tool.

Creating a database with SSMS 2014

Here are the steps for creating databases with SQL Server 2014 Management Studio:

1. Launch SQL Server 2014 Management Studio.

2. In **Object Explorer**, right-click on the Databases folder and select **New Database** from the context menu. This opens the **New Database** window.

3. In the **General** page of the **New Database** window, type in CH02_04 in the **Database name** textbox.

4. On the same page, select the owner of the database. By default, the user who creates the database is set as the owner of the database.

5. In the **Database files** section, configure the data and transaction log file settings for this database. For the purposes of this demonstration, we will add a user-defined filegroup called CH02_04FG that contains one secondary data file named CH02_04Data02, as shown in the following screenshot:

6. To change database options, select **Options**. Change options as necessary and then click on **OK** to create a database, as shown in the following screenshot:

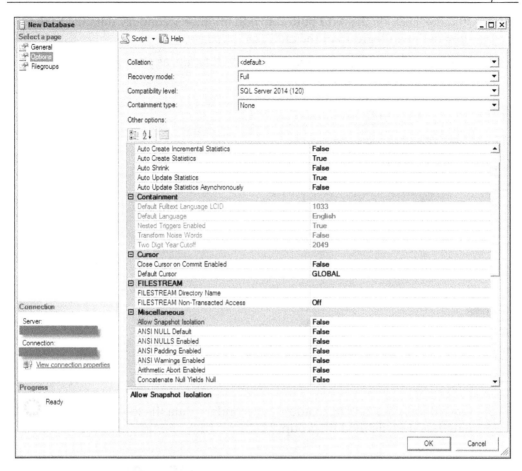

Modifying a database with SSMS 2014

This section illustrates how you can modify an existing SQL Server database using SQL Server 2014 Management Studio. Here are the steps for modifying an existing SQL Server database using SQL Server 2014 Management Studio:

1. In **Object Explorer**, expand the `Databases` folder.

2. Right-click on the `CH02_04` database and select **Properties**.

3. In there, click on the **Add** button to add another secondary data file to the user-defined filegroup of the CH02_04 database.

4. Configure the settings for this secondary data file, as shown in the following screenshot:

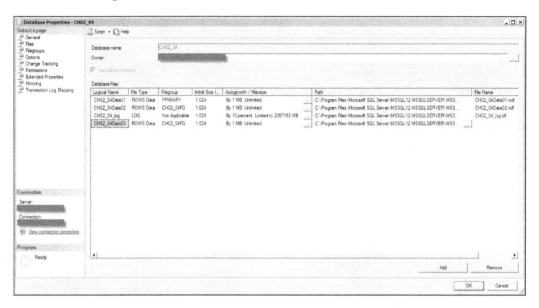

5. Once done, click on **OK** to add this secondary data file to the CH02_04 database user-defined filegroup.

Dropping a database with SSMS 2014

To drop a database, use the following steps:

1. To drop a database, right-click on the name of the database you want to delete and then choose **Delete** from the shortcut menu. This opens the **Delete Object** window, as shown in the following screenshot:

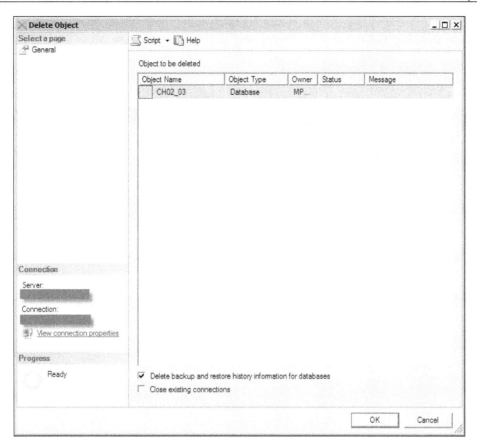

2. Click on **OK** to drop the database from the SQL Server instance.

Creating and managing database schemas

A schema is a logical container that groups objects of similar scope or ownership together. By default, the database owner (dbo) schema is automatically created in a SQL Server database. Unless you specify otherwise, all SQL Server user objects are created in the database owner (dbo) schema. You can define different default schemas for each user of the database. When you create a user database, SQL Server automatically creates these schemas: sys, dbo, INFORMATION_SCHEMA, and guest.

You can query the `sys.schemas` system catalog view to see the schemas defined for the database. The following is the syntax to query this system catalog:

```
SELECT * FROM sys.schemas
```

You can also use SQL Server Management Studio 2014 to list the schemas defined for the database. To list the schemas defined for the database in SQL Server 2014 Management Studio, use the following steps:

1. In **Object Explorer**, expand the `Databases` folder.
2. Next, select the database and expand the `Security` folder.
3. Finally, expand the `Schemas` folder to list the schemas defined for the database.

Managing schemas using T-SQL DDL statements

You can use the `CREATE SCHEMA` statement to create a schema. The following is the basic syntax of this command:

```
CREATE SCHEMA schema_name
AUTHORIZATION user_or_role
```

We use the `ALTER SCHEMA` statement to transfer objects from one schema to another. The following is the basic syntax of this command:

```
ALTER SCHEMA schema_name
  TRANSFER [ <entity_type> :: ] securable_name [;]
```

To delete a schema, we use the `DROP SCHEMA` statement as follows:

```
DROP SCHEMA schema_name
```

Managing schemas using SSMS 2014

The following are the steps to create a schema from SQL Server 2014 Management Studio:

1. In the **Object Explorer** window, expand the `Databases` folder.
2. Next, expand the database in which you want to create a schema.
3. Expand the `Security` folder and then right-click on the `Schemas` folder.

4. Choose **New Schema** and then enter the schema name and owner. You can view and select from a list of available owners by clicking on the **Search** button in the **New Schema** dialog box.

5. Click on **OK** to create a schema.

To delete a schema, right-click on the schema and choose **Delete**.

Creating and managing tables

After you have created the database, the next step is to create tables. Tables are objects that store and organize data within a database. SQL Server provides the following types of tables:

- **Temporary tables**: These exist within the `tempdb` database. These tables do not exist permanently. Instead, temporary tables have a life and limited accessibility, which differ according to their type. You can create two types of temporary tables: local and global. The name of the local temporary table must begin with a single number sign (#) and the name of the global temporary table must begin with two number signs (##). Local temporary tables are only available in the user session that created the table. Therefore, SQL Server removes the local temporary table when the user session ends. On the other hand, global temporary tables are available for all user sessions after its creation. SQL Server removes the global temporary table once all user sessions that refer to it are disconnected.

- **System tables**: These store data about SQL Server 2014 and its components. SQL Server does not allow you to directly update the data of system tables.

- **User-defined tables**: These are standard tables that contain user data. You can create up to 2,147,483,647 tables per user database.

- **Partitioned tables**: These are a type of user-defined tables whose data is horizontally divided into distinct units and spread across one or more filegroups in a database. Partitioned tables make the large tables and indexes more manageable because you can manage them separately. By default, SQL Server 2014 supports up to 15,000 partitions.

- **File tables**: Since SQL 2012, the SQL Server database engine lets you save files and directories in a SQL Server database. The FileTable feature builds on top of SQL Server FILESTREAM technology. File table has a fixed schema, and every row in this table represents a file or directory. Files can be loaded in bulk and updated and managed in T-SQL like any other column. SQL Server also supports the backup and restore operations on file tables. File tables allow files and similar objects to be stored in the SQL Server database, but allow access to them as if they were stored in the filesystem. All this is possible without any changes to client applications.

- **Memory-optimized tables**: SQL Server 2014 allows you to create memory-optimized tables within a database. It is one of the key new performance-related architectural enhancements to the SQL Server 2014 database engine. The benefit of memory-optimized tables is to improve the performance of OLTP applications, as all the data for memory-optimized tables resides in memory. All transactions on memory-optimized OLTP tables are fully **atomic, consistent, isolated, and durable (ACID)**.

Creating and modifying tables

You can use either Transact-SQL DDL statements or SQL Server Management Studio to create and modify tables. In the following sections, we will discuss these options.

Creating and modifying tables with T-SQL DDL statements

In this section, you will learn how to create and manage tables using T-SQL DDL statements.

Creating a table with T-SQL DDL statements

We use the CREATE TABLE statement to create tables within a database. The following is the basic syntax for this command:

```
CREATE TABLE [[database_name.]schema.]table_name
(column_name data_type | [column_definition] |
[computed_column], [table_constraint])
[ON filegroup | partition_scheme | DEFAULT]
[TEXTIMAGE_ON filegroup|DEFAULT]
[FILESTREAM_ON partition_scheme_name | filegroup | default]
    [ WITH ( <table_option> [ ,...n ] ) ]
[;]
```

For example, enter and execute the following T-SQL code in the query editor to create a `Book_Info` table within a CH02_03 database:

```
USE [CH02_03];
GO
CREATE TABLE Book_Info
    (
        Book_ID SMALLINT ,
        Book_Name VARCHAR(20) ,
        Description VARCHAR(30) ,
        Price [SMALLMONEY] ,
        Author_ID [int]
    )
ON CH02_FG1;
GO
```

To create memory-optimized tables, we must first create a MEMORY_OPTIMIZED_DATA filegroup within a database. For example, to create a MEMORY_OPTIMIZED_DATA filegroup in the CH02_03 database, we enter and execute the following T-SQL code:

```
USE [master];
GO

ALTER DATABASE [CH02_03]
ADD FILEGROUP [CH02_FGMO]
CONTAINS MEMORY_OPTIMIZED_DATA;
GO
```

Next, run the following code to add a database file to the CH02_03 database memory-optimized file group (CH02_FGMO):

```
USE [master];
GO

ALTER DATABASE [CH02_03]
ADD FILE (NAME = 'CH02_03_MemoryOptimized', FILENAME =
'C:\SQLData\CH02_03_MO.ndf')
TO FILEGROUP CH02_FGMO
GO
```

Finally, enter and execute the following T-SQL code to create a memory-optimized version of the `Book_Info_MO` table within the CH02_03 database:

```
USE [CH02_03];
GO

CREATE TABLE Book_Info_MO
```

```
    (
        Book_ID SMALLINT NOT NULL,
        Book_Name VARCHAR(20),
        Description VARCHAR(30),
        Price [SMALLMONEY],
        Author_ID [int],
        CONSTRAINT [PK_Book_Info_ID] PRIMARY KEY
        NONCLUSTERED HASH (Book_ID) WITH (BUCKET_COUNT = 2000))
        WITH (MEMORY_OPTIMIZED = ON, DURABILITY = SCHEMA_AND_DATA);
GO
```

Modifying a table with T-SQL DDL statements

We use the ALTER TABLE statement to modify an existing table. The following is the basic syntax for this command:

```
ALTER TABLE [[database.]schema.]table_name
[ADD | ALTER | DROP column_information]
[ADD | DROP constraint_information [index_properties]]
[WITH CHECK | NOCHECK CONSTRAINT constraint_name | ALL]
[ENABLE | DISABLE TRIGGER trigger_name | ALL]
[SWITCH partition_information] [;]
```

For example, to add a Topic_ID column to the Book_Info table, we execute the following T-SQL code:

```
USE [CH02_03];
GO

ALTER TABLE [Book_Info]
ADD [Topic_ID] INT NOT NULL;
GO
```

Dropping a table with T-SQL DDL statements

We use the DROP TABLE statement to delete the table from the SQL Server database. The basic syntax for this is as follows:

```
DROP TABLE table_name
```

For example, enter and execute the following T-SQL code to drop the `Book_Info_MO` table from the `CH02_03` database:

```
USE [CH02_03];
GO
DROP TABLE Book_Info_MO;
GO
```

Creating and modifying tables with SSMS 2014

You can use SQL Server 2014 Management Studio to create and modify tables. In this section, we will cover this GUI tool.

Creating a table with SSMS 2014

Here are the steps to create tables with SQL Server 2014 Management Studio:

1. Launch SQL Server 2014 Management Studio.

2. In **Object Explorer**, expand the `Databases` folder and then click on the `Tables` folder and select **New Table** from the menu. This launches the table designer in SSMS 2014.

3. Use the **Table**, **Properties**, and **Column Properties** panes to define some basic information about the table, as shown in the following screenshot:

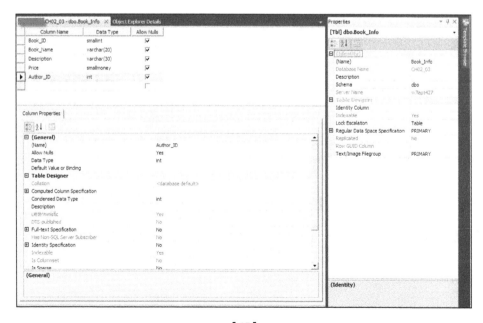

4. Click on the **Save** button.

5. Type in the table name in the textbox on the **Choose Name** window and then click on **OK** to save the table.

Modifying a table with SSMS 2014

Here are the steps to modify an existing database table with SQL Server 2014 Management Studio:

1. Launch SQL Server 2014 Management Studio.

2. In **Object Explorer**, expand the Databases folder and then expand the Tables folder.

3. Right-click on the table you want to modify and then select **Design** from the menu. This opens the table designer.

4. After making changes to the table design, click on the **Save** button to save the changes.

Deleting a table with SSMS 2014

To delete a table, use the following steps:

1. Launch SQL Server 2014 Management Studio.

2. In **Object Explorer**, expand the Databases folder and then expand the Tables folder.

3. Right-click on the table you want to delete and choose **Delete** from the menu. Click on **OK** to delete the table.

Grant, deny, and revoke permissions to securables

You can use SQL Server Management Studio or the T-SQL DCL statements to grant, revoke, and deny permissions to securables.

Grant, deny, and revoke permissions to securables with T-SQL DCL statements

In this section, we will use T-SQL DCL statements to grant, deny and revoke permissions.

Granting permissions to securables with T-SQL DCL statements

We use the GRANT keyword to grant permissions to securables. The basic syntax for the GRANT statement is as follows:

```
GRANT permission [,...n]
TO <grantee_principal> [,...n] [WITH GRANT OPTION]
[AS <grantor_principal>]
```

We use WITH GRANT OPTION when we want the user to grant the same permission to other logins.

For example, to grant Bob the SELECT permission WITH GRANT OPTION on the Book_Info table, you execute the following code:

```
USE [CH02_03];
GO

GRANT SELECT ON [dbo].[Book_Info] TO [Bob]
WITH GRANT OPTION;
GO
```

Denying permissions to securables with T-SQL DCL statements

We use the DENY keyword to prevent a user from performing certain actions. The basic syntax for this command is as follows:

```
DENY permission [,...n]
TO <grantee_principal> [,...n]
[CASCADE]
[AS <grantor_principal>]
```

We can specify the CASCADE option when we want to deny the permission to the specified principal and to all the other principals to which the principal granted the permission.

For example, enter and execute the following T-SQL code to deny Bob the UPDATE permission on the Book_Info table:

```
USE [CH02_03];
GO

DENY UPDATE ON [dbo].[Book_Info] TO [Bob];
GO
```

Revoking permissions to securables with T-SQL DCL statements

We use the REVOKE keyword to remove the permission assigned using the GRANT or DENY keyword. The following is the basic syntax for this command:

```
REVOKE [GRANT OPTION FOR] permission [,...n]
{ TO | FROM } <grantee_principal> [,...n]
[CASCADE]
[AS <grantor_principal>
```

Managing permissions using SSMS 2014

You can manage permissions using SQL Server Management Studio. For example, the following are the steps to grant, deny, or revoke user permissions to securables via SSMS 2014:

1. Launch SQL Server 2014 Management Studio.
2. In **Object Explorer**, expand the Databases folder and then expand the Tables folder.
3. Right-click on the table and choose **Properties**.
4. Click on **Permissions** and then select a user or role to which you want to assign a permission.
5. In the explicit permissions list, check **Grant**, **With Grant**, or **Deny** for the appropriate permission. To revoke a permission, uncheck the box.
6. Click on **OK** to complete this action.

Summary

In this chapter, you learned about the Transact-SQL DDL, DML, and DCL language elements. You also understood the purpose of SQL Server 2014 system databases. We then covered the purpose of database recovery models. We used the DDL language CREATE statement to create databases, schemas, and tables. We then used the DDL language ALTER statement to modify databases, schemas, and tables. We also used the DDL language DROP statement to delete databases, schemas, and tables. Finally, you learned how to set permissions on SQL Server objects using the DCL language GRANT, DENY, and REVOKE statements.

3
Data Retrieval Using Transact-SQL Statements

The primary purpose of creating databases and tables in SQL Server is to store data and make that data available to users and application queries. Like any other **Relational Database Management System (RDBMS)**, retrieval of data from a SQL Server database is a relatively straightforward task. In this chapter, you will learn how to get data from the databases using the Transact-SQL (T-SQL) SELECT statement. After reading through the chapter, you will be able to understand the following:

- Transact-SQL SELECT, FROM, and WHERE clauses
- Use a Transact-SQL function in a query
- Multiple table queries using UNION, EXCEPT, INTERSECT, and JOINs
- Use subqueries and CTEs to perform advanced queries
- Organizing, grouping, and pivoting data
- Use of the Transact-SQL analytic window functions

This chapter contains a large number of example T-SQL queries, all of which require the AdventureWorks2012 database, which is available for download from http://msftdbprodsamples.codeplex.com/downloads/get/478214.

After attaching the AdventureWorks2012 database to your SQL Server instance, enter and execute the following Transact-SQL in SSMS 2014 to set its compatibility level to SQL Server 2014:

```
USE [master];
GO

ALTER DATABASE [AdventureWorks2012] SET
COMPATIBILITY_LEVEL = 120;
GO
```

Understanding Transact-SQL SELECT, FROM, and WHERE clauses

In this section, you will learn how to use the Transact-SQL SELECT, FROM, and WHERE clauses to retrieve the data you need from the SQL Server databases.

The SELECT statement

The SELECT statement is the most frequently used Transact-SQL statement. We use the SELECT statement for the following purposes:

- To query specific data from the selected database tables
- To assign a value to local variables
- To call a function

We often see SELECT statements within programming objects (such as views, stored procedures, functions, batches, and **common table expressions (CTEs)**). We also use SELECT statements to run ad hoc queries, most often through an SSMS 2014 query window. The SELECT statement has several clauses, most of which are optional. The following is the general syntax of the SELECT statement:

```
SELECT [TOP(n)|TOP(n) PERCENT] [ALL|DISTINCT] select_list
[INTO[[database.]owner.]table_name]
FROM[[[database.]owner.]table_name|view_name|UDF]
[WHERE search_conditions]
[GROUP BY aggregate_free_expression]
[HAVING search_conditions]
[ORDER BY table_or_view_and_column]
[COMPUTE row_aggregate(column_name)]
[BY column_name]]
[FOR for_options]
[OPTION (query_hint)] [;]
```

The select_list parameter is the list of expressions (such as numeric computation, constants, functions, aliases, and subqueries) or columns in the SELECT clause that you want to return in the query result set. We can use asterisk (*) as a wildcard character in the select_list parameter of the SELECT statement to return all columns from the selected tables. For example, the following query returns all columns from the Sales.Currency table in the AdventureWorks2012 database:

```
SELECT  *
FROM    [Sales].[Currency];
```

However, you should avoid using the asterisk (*) wildcard character in `select_list`; instead, provide a full list of columns needed for the query, because SQL Server resolves the column list each time the SELECT statement is executed. Moreover, if we use SELECT * in the T-SQL code, the SELECT statement might generate an error due to changes in the schemas of the underlying tables. To display the values in CurrencyCode and Name from the Sales.Currency table, run the following code:

```
SELECT   [CurrencyCode] ,
         [Name]
FROM     [Sales].[Currency];
```

The FROM clause

The purpose of the FROM clause in the SELECT statement is to identify the data sources for a query. For example, in the previous example, we used the FROM clause in the SELECT statement to specify the Sales.Currency table as a data source for the query.

The WHERE clause

The WHERE clause is used to specify the query criteria, so that only the required subset of data is returned in the result set. For example, suppose that you want to write a query to return all the currency codes that begin with the A character. To accomplish this, we include the WHERE clause in the preceding query as follows:

```
SELECT   [CurrencyCode] ,
         [Name]
FROM     [Sales].[Currency]
WHERE    [CurrencyCode] LIKE 'A%';
```

The WHERE clause always comes after the FROM clause and can include conditions that use the following:

- Comparison operators (= (equal to), <> (not equal to), != (not equal to), > (greater than), !> (not greater than), < (less than), !< (not less than), >= (greater than or equal to), and <= (less than or equal to))
- Subqueries and JOINs
- The LIKE operator for wildcard searches
- The BETWEEN operator for searching ranges of data
- The IN and NOT IN operators to match any one value from a list of values
- The EXISTS and NOT EXISTS keywords to check whether a value or record exists in the result set
- The IS and IS NOT operators to search for NULLs

Using T-SQL functions in the query

As mentioned earlier, we can also use the functions in your SELECT statements. SQL Server 2014 comes with many built-in functions (also known as system functions), and also lets you create user-defined functions. The functions are either deterministic or nondeterministic. The deterministic functions return the same value every time, while nondeterministic functions might return different values each time based on the values of their specified input parameters. The SQL Server 2014 built-in functions belong to one of the following categories:

- Aggregate functions
- Configuration functions
- Cursor functions
- Date and time functions
- Mathematical functions
- Metadata functions
- Other functions
- Rowset functions
- Security functions
- String functions
- System statistical functions

Aggregate functions

Aggregate functions operate on a group of rows and return a single summarizing value. The SQL Server 2014 aggregate functions include AVG, MIN, MAX, SUM, CHECKSUM_AGG, COUNT, COUNT_BIG, STDEV, STDEVP, GROUPING, GROUPING_ID, VAR, and VARP.

In the following query, I used the AVG function to calculate the average unit price for all orders:

```
SELECT AVG(OrderQty * UnitPrice) AS [Avg]
FROM   [Sales].[SalesOrderDetail];
```

In the following query, I used the COUNT function to count the number of orders where ProductID is 777:

```
SELECT   COUNT(*)
FROM   [Sales].[SalesOrderDetail]
WHERE    ProductID = 777;
```

Configuration functions

Configuration functions return the current option configuration settings. These are the SQL Server 2014 configuration functions: @@DATEFIRST, @@OPTIONS, @@DBTS, @@REMSERVER, @@LANGID, @@SERVERNAME, @@LANGUAGE, @@SERVICENAME, @@LOCK_TIMEOUT, @@SPID, @@MAX_CONNECTIONS, @@TEXTSIZE, @@VERSION, @@MAX_PRECISION, and @@NESTLEVEL.

The following query returns the SQL Server name and version information:

```
SELECT  @@SERVERNAME ,
        @@VERSION;
```

Cursor functions

We use cursor functions to return information about cursors. The SQL Server 2014 cursor functions include @@CURSOR_ROWS, CURSOR_STATUS, and @@FETCH_STATUS. Cursor functions do not return the same value each time.

Date and time functions

Date and time functions are used to retrieve and manipulate information about dates and times. These are the SQL Server 2014 date and time functions: SYSDATETIME, SYSDATETIMEOFFSET, SYSUTCDATETIME, CURRENT_TIMESTAMP, GETDATE, GETUTCDATE, DATENAME, DATEPART, DAY, MONTH, YEAR, DATEFROMPARTS, DATETIME2FROMPARTS, DATETIMEFROMPARTS, DATETIMEOFFSETFROMPARTS, SMALLDATETIMEFROMPARTS, TIMEFROMPARTS, DATEDIFF, DATEADD, EOMONTH, SWITCHOFFSET, TODATETIMEOFFSET, and ISDATE.

To return the current system date and time, we either use the GETDATE or CURRENT_TIMESTAMP function as follows:

```
SELECT  GETDATE() ,
        CURRENT_TIMESTAMP;
```

Or, to find the number of days between two specified dates, we use the DATEDIFF function. For example, enter and execute the following to return the total number of days since January 1, 2014:

```
SELECT DATEDIFF(DAY, '01-01-2014', CURRENT_TIMESTAMP);
```

Mathematical functions

We use mathematical functions to perform mathematical operations based on the input values specified as parameters to these functions. The SQL Server 2014 mathematical functions are ABS, DEGREES, RAND, ACOS, EXP, ROUND, ASIN, FLOOR, SIGN, ATAN, LOG, SIN, ATN2, LOG10, SQRT, CEILING, PI, SQUARE, COS, POWER, TAN, COT, and RADIANS.

Run the following code to round off the AvergateRate and EndOfDayRate columns of the Sales.CurrencyRate table to one decimal place:

```
SELECT    [FromCurrencyCode] ,
          [ToCurrencyCode] ,
          ROUND([AverageRate], 1) ,
          ROUND([EndOfDayRate], 1)
FROM      [Sales].[CurrencyRate];
```

Metadata functions

We use metadata functions to return information about databases, the files and filegroups associated with them, and their objects. A detailed discussion of metadata functions is beyond the scope of this chapter.

To determine the date when the statistics where last updated for each statistics object that exists for the tables, indexes, and indexed views in the database, we execute the sys.stats system catalog view with the STATS_DATE() function as follows:

```
SELECT    OBJECT_NAME(object_id),
          [name] AS [StatisticName],
          STATS_DATE([object_id], [stats_id])
FROM      sys.stats;
```

Rowset functions

The rowset functions return an object that can be used in place of a table or view name in a Transact-SQL statement. The rowset functions include OPENDATASOURCE, OPENROWSET, OPENQUERY, and OPENXML.

Security functions

The security functions are used to return the security information about users and roles. The information returned is useful for managing security. A detailed discussion of the security functions is beyond the scope of this chapter.

String functions

String functions are used to manipulate string data. All strings specified in a string function must be enclosed in single quotes.

The following uses the CONCAT function to concatenate the FirstName, MiddleName, and LastName columns of the Person.Person table:

```
SELECT   CONCAT([FirstName] + SPACE(1) ,
                [MiddleName] + SPACE(1),
                [LastName])
FROM     [Person].[Person];
```

System statistical functions

We use system statistical functions to return information about connections and resource usage since SQL Server was last restarted. For example, we can use the @@CONNECTIONS function to return successful or unsuccessful connection attempts since SQL Server was last started. Have a look at the following query:

```
SELECT @@CONNECTIONS;
```

> For a full list of Transact-SQL deterministic and nondeterministic functions and their parameters, refer to the *Deterministic and Nondeterministic Functions* topic at http://msdn.microsoft.com/en-us/library/ms178091.aspx.

Multiple table queries using UNION, EXCEPT, INTERSECT, and JOINs

So far in this book, we have seen queries that only retrieve data from a single table. However, in the real world, it is very unlikely that you will write queries that only refer to a single table. In practice, the requirement might be to retrieve data from multiple tables. SQL Server 2014 provides several options to create queries that return data from multiple tables. In this section, we will explore these options.

The UNION operator

The UNION operator is used to combine the result sets of two or more SELECT statements to generate a single result set. The following is the basic syntax for using the UNION operator:

```
select_statement UNION [ALL] select_statement
[UNION [ALL] select_statement [...n]]
```

The key point to remember is that all statements combined using the UNION operator must have the same number of columns and must have compatible data types. The column names of the first SELECT statement are used as headings for the result set.

 By default, the UNION operator removes duplicate rows from the result set. If you do not want to remove duplicate rows, specify the ALL keyword. UNION ALL is faster than UNION because it requires less backend processing for the union operation. This is because the UNION clause also adds an additional sorting operation to remove duplicate rows from two or more SELECT statements. Therefore, it is better to use UNION ALL, where possible.

Have a look at the following Venn diagram to get a better understanding of UNION and UNION ALL operators:

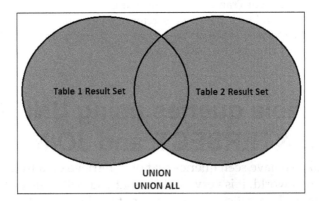

For example, the following query returns all products associated with a purchase order and all products associated with a sales order:

```
SELECT    [ProductID],
          [UnitPrice],
          [OrderQty]
FROM      [Purchasing].[PurchaseOrderDetail]
UNION
SELECT    [ProductID],
```

```
            [UnitPrice],
            [OrderQty]
    FROM    [Sales].[SalesOrderDetail];
```

We will run the following query to keep duplicates:

```
    SELECT  [ProductID] ,
            [UnitPrice] ,
            [OrderQty]
    FROM    [Purchasing].[PurchaseOrderDetail]
    UNION ALL
    SELECT  [ProductID] ,
            [UnitPrice] ,
            [OrderQty]
    FROM    [Sales].[SalesOrderDetail];
```

The EXCEPT operator

The EXCEPT operator compares the results of two SELECT statements and returns only distinct rows from the first SELECT statement result set that do not exist in the second SELECT statement result set. The following is the basic syntax for using the EXCEPT operator:

```
    select_statement EXCEPT select_statement
```

Like the UNION operator, all statements combined using the EXCEPT operator must have compatible data types and the same number of columns. Have a look at the following diagram:

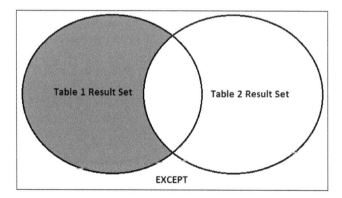

For example, let's rewrite the preceding query to return only distinct ProductID, UnitPrice, and OrderQty values of those products associated with the purchase orders that do not have an associated sales order. Have a look at the following code:

```
SELECT    [ProductID] ,
          [UnitPrice] ,
          [OrderQty]
FROM      [Purchasing] . [PurchaseOrderDetail]
EXCEPT
SELECT    [ProductID] ,
          [UnitPrice] ,
          [OrderQty]
FROM      [Sales] . [SalesOrderDetail] ;
```

The INTERSECT operator

The INTERSECT operator compares the results of two SELECT statements and only returns distinct rows from the first SELECT statement result set that also exist in the second SELECT statement result set. The general syntax for the INTERSECT statement is as follows:

```
select_statement INTERSECT select_statement
```

Similar to the UNION and EXCEPT operators, the INTERSECT operator has the same SELECT list restrictions. The following diagram will help you understand the INTERSECT operator:

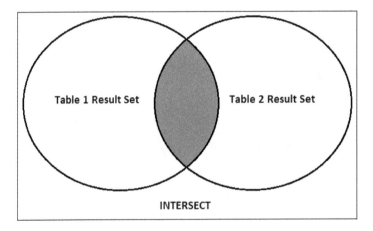

For example, to find out which currency codes exist in both the `Sales.Currency` table and the `Sales.CurrencyRate` table, we need to retrieve the distinct list of currency codes, for which we will run the following query:

```
SELECT   [CurrencyCode]
FROM     [Sales].[Currency]
INTERSECT
SELECT   [ToCurrencyCode]
FROM     [Sales].[CurrencyRate];
```

The JOIN operator

The `JOIN` operator is used to join columns from multiple tables and return them in a single result set. The JOINs often use foreign key relationships to join multiple related tables. The basic syntax for the `JOIN` operator is as follows:

```
SELECT select_list
FROM table_or_view
[INNER | LEFT | RIGHT | FULL | OUTER] JOIN table_or_view
ON (join_condition)
```

The following are the four main types of joins: inner joins, outer joins, cross joins, and self joins. In this section, we will discuss these join types.

Using INNER JOIN

Include only those records in the result set that satisfy the join condition. Therefore, inner joins are also called equi-joins. For example, the following query uses `INNER JOIN` to retrieve all the employees' names, titles, and current department information:

```
SELECT   p.[Title] ,
p.[FirstName] + SPACE(1)
+ p.[MiddleName] + SPACE(1)
+ p.[LastName] AS [FullName] ,
e.[JobTitle] ,
d.[Name] AS [Department] ,
d.[GroupName] ,
dhist.[StartDate]
FROM     [HumanResources].[Employee] e
INNER JOIN [HumanResources].[EmployeeDepartmentHistory] dhist
ON e.[BusinessEntityID] = dhist.[BusinessEntityID]
AND dhist.[EndDate] IS NULL
INNER JOIN [Person].[Person] p
ON p.[BusinessEntityID] = e.[BusinessEntityID]
INNER JOIN [HumanResources].[Department] d
ON dhist.[DepartmentID] = d.[DepartmentID];
```

Using outer joins

The outer joins return all rows, whether or not they satisfy the join conditions. There are three basic outer join types: LEFT OUTER JOIN (left join), RIGHT OUTER JOIN (right join), and FULL OUTER JOIN (full join).

Using LEFT OUTER JOIN

The LEFT OUTER JOIN operator returns all rows from the left table named in the LEFT OUTER JOIN clause. If there is no matching row in the table to the right, SQL Server displays the values of the right table as NULLs. For example, the following query uses LEFT OUTER JOIN to retrieve an employee's name and title, regardless of whether they have a phone, an e-mail ID, and additional contact information:

```
SELECT   p.[Title] ,
p.[FirstName] + SPACE(1)
+ p.[MiddleName] + SPACE(1)
+ p.[LastName] AS [FullName] ,
pp.[PhoneNumber] ,
pt.[Name] AS [PhoneNumberType] ,
ea.[EmailAddress] ,
p.[AdditionalContactInfo]
FROM [HumanResources].[Employee] e
INNER JOIN [Person].[Person] p
ON p.[BusinessEntityID] = e.[BusinessEntityID]
LEFT OUTER JOIN [Person].[EmailAddress] ea
ON p.[BusinessEntityID] = ea.[BusinessEntityID]
LEFT OUTER JOIN [Person].[PersonPhone] pp
ON pp.[BusinessEntityID] = p.[BusinessEntityID]
LEFT OUTER JOIN [Person].[PhoneNumberType] pt
ON pp.[PhoneNumberTypeID] = pt.[PhoneNumberTypeID] ;
```

Using RIGHT OUTER JOIN

The RIGHT OUTER JOIN operator returns all rows from the right table named in the RIGHT OUTER JOIN clause. If there is no matching row in the left table, SQL Server displays the values of the left table as NULLs. For example, the following query uses RIGHT OUTER JOIN to return the list of all products, regardless of whether there is a special discount associated with the product:

```
SELECT   p.[ProductID] ,
p.[Name] ,
so.[SpecialOfferID] ,
so.[Description] ,
so.[DiscountPct] ,
so.[Type] ,
so.[Category] ,
```

```
        so.[StartDate] ,
        so.[EndDate] ,
        so.[MinQty] ,
        so.[MaxQty]
FROM [Sales].[SpecialOfferProduct] sop
RIGHT OUTER JOIN [Sales].[SpecialOffer] so
ON so.[SpecialOfferID] = sop.[SpecialOfferID]
RIGHT OUTER JOIN [Production].[Product] p
ON p.[ProductID] = sop.[ProductID];
```

Using FULL OUTER JOIN

The FULL OUTER JOIN operator returns all rows from both tables. If there are no matches between the right and left rows, SQL Server displays the missing values as NULLs. In other words, FULL OUTER JOIN acts as a combination of LEFT OUTER JOIN and RIGHT OUTER JOIN.

Using CROSS JOIN

The CROSS JOIN operator returns all rows from the table to the left. Each row in the table to the left is combined with all rows in the table to the right. This is also known as a Cartesian product. The cross join does not have an ON clause. The following is an example of a cross join:

```
SELECT  c.* ,
        crc.*
FROM [Sales].[Currency] c
     CROSS JOIN [Sales].[CountryRegionCurrency] crc;
```

Using self joins

In self join, you join a table to itself in order to find the rows in a table that have values in common with other rows of the table. Self joins are rarely used in a normalized database. Create a table alias to reference the table multiple times in the same query. We can also use a WHERE clause to eliminate cases where a row matches itself.

Subqueries

A subquery is a query that is nested inside a SELECT, INSERT, UPDATE, or DELETE statement, or inside another subquery. Subqueries are often used in situations where a query depends on the results of another query. SQL Server supports noncorrelated and correlated subqueries.

In a noncorrelated subquery, the inner query is independent and gets evaluated first, then passes results to the outer query. A noncorrelated (independent) subquery can be independently evaluated and relies only on its own SELECT clause for instructions.

In a correlated subquery, the outer query provides values for the dependant inner subquery evaluation. SQL Server passes the subquery results back to the outer query for evaluation. A correlated (dependant) subquery receives values from the outer SELECT statement.

> Subqueries are useful for solving complex data retrieval and modification problems; however, this method is often less efficient than performing a join operation.

Typically, the statements that include subqueries take one of three forms. The first form is to use a comparison operator in the WHERE clause, as follows:

```
WHERE expression comparison_operator [ANY | ALL] (subquery)
```

When ALL is specified, SQL Server evaluates the expression as true if it is true for either all rows or none of the rows. When ANY is specified, SQL Server evaluates the expression to true if the expression is true for at least one row of a subquery.

In the second form, we use the IN keyword (or NOT IN) in the WHERE clause of the outside query as follows:

```
WHERE expression [NOT] IN (subquery)
```

In the third form, we use the EXISTS (or NOT EXISTS) keyword in the WHERE clause as follows:

```
WHERE expression [NOT] EXISTS (subquery)
```

Examples of subqueries

The following query returns the names of all employees who have a valid e-mail address:

```
SELECT   [Title] ,
         [FirstName] ,
         [MiddleName] ,
         [LastName]
FROM     [Person].[Person] p
WHERE    EXISTS ( SELECT *
                  FROM   [Person].[EmailAddress] e
                  WHERE  p.[BusinessEntityID] =
e.[BusinessEntityID] );
```

To return a list of all customers who live in territories that are not covered by any salesperson, we will execute the following T-SQL code:

```
SELECT   *
FROM     [Sales].[Customer]
WHERE    [TerritoryID] <> ANY (SELECT   [TerritoryID]
                      FROM      [Sales].[SalesPerson]);
```

The following query finds the `CustomerID` and `AccountNumber` values of all customers who live in Europe:

```
SELECT   [CustomerID] ,
         [AccountNumber]
FROM     [Sales].[Customer]
WHERE    [TerritoryID] IN (
         SELECT   [TerritoryID]
         FROM     [Sales].[SalesTerritory]
         WHERE    [Group] = 'Europe');
```

Common Table Expressions

A common table expression (CTE) is a temporary result set that your query can reference. You can use a CTE just as you would any other table. However, when the query ends, the CTE is deleted from the memory. We also use CTEs to create recursive queries, simplify complex query logic, and create multiple references of the same table.

To create a CTE, use a `WITH` clause outside the `SELECT` statement. The following is the basic syntax of a CTE:

```
WITH cte_name ([[(column_name [,...n])])
AS
(CTE_query_definition)
```

The following is an explanation of the arguments of the CTE syntax:

- `cte_name`: This is the name of the CTE you have referenced in the query

- `column_name`: This is the name of the column; note that it is an optional argument

The following is an example of the structure of a CTE:

```
WITH    cteSalesPerson ( [SalesPersonID], [FullName],
[TerritoryName], [SalesQuota], [Bonus], [CommissionPct],
[SalesYTD], [SalesLastYear] )
AS ( SELECT    sp1.[BusinessEntityID] ,
sp2.[FirstName] + SPACE(1) + sp2.[LastName] ,
st.[Name] ,
sp1.[SalesQuota] ,
sp1.[Bonus] ,
sp1.[CommissionPct] ,
sp1.[SalesYTD] ,
sp1.[SalesLastYear]
FROM [Sales].[SalesPerson] sp1
INNER JOIN [Sales].[vSalesPerson] sp2
ON sp2.[BusinessEntityID] = sp1.[BusinessEntityID]
INNER JOIN [Sales].[SalesTerritory] st
ON st.[TerritoryID] = sp1.[TerritoryID]
WHERE sp1.[TerritoryID] IS NOT NULL
)
SELECT   *
FROM     cteSalesPerson;
```

The query inside the CTE returns every salesperson's current and previous years' sales figures. The following are the columns returned by this CTE query: SalesPersonID, FullName, TerritoryName, SalesQuota, Bonus, CommissionPct, SalesYTD, and SalesLastYear.

Organizing and grouping data

We can use the SELECT statement and its clauses and keywords to organize and summarize data. In this section, we will cover these clauses.

The ORDER BY clause

By default, when you query the data in a table with no clustered index, SQL Server does not guarantee the order in which data is returned and returns rows in a random order. If the table has a clustered index, SQL Server returns the rows in a clustered index order. Therefore, we use the ORDER BY clause in your SELECT statements to sort the data returned by the query based on the columns' sort order specified in the ORDER BY clause. The ORDER BY clause guarantees the order in which data is returned.

For example, to display a sales representative's sales-related information ordered by the FirstName and LastName values, we would run the following query:

```
SELECT  *
FROM    [Sales].[vSalesPerson]
ORDER BY [FirstName] ASC,
         [LastName] ASC;
```

The GROUP BY clause

The GROUP BY clause is used to divide the table into groups and return a row for each group. We use the GROUP BY clause with aggregate functions to produce summary values for each set. The general syntax of the GROUP BY clause is as follows:

```
SELECT select_list
FROM[[[database.]owner.]table_name|view_name|UDF]
[WHERE search_conditions]
[GROUP BY [ALL] aggregate_free_expression
[, aggregate_free_expression...]]
[HAVING search_conditions]
```

Each column in the SELECT clause must either be an aggregate function or be included in the GROUP BY clause. For example, to retrieve the number of customers in each territory, you would use the following query:

```
SELECT  st.[Name] ,
        COUNT(c.[CustomerID]) [TotalCustomer]
FROM    [Sales].[Customer] c
        INNER JOIN [Sales].[SalesTerritory] st
        ON st.[TerritoryID] = c.[TerritoryID]
GROUP BY st.[Name];
```

The HAVING clause

We use the HAVING clause to set the search conditions that restrict the groups returned. For example, the following query returns only those territories in which the number of customers is less than 1,000:

```
SELECT  st.[Name] ,
        COUNT(c.[CustomerID]) [TotalCustomer]
FROM    [Sales].[Customer] c
        INNER JOIN [Sales].[SalesTerritory] st
        ON st.[TerritoryID] = c.[TerritoryID]
GROUP BY st.[Name]
HAVING (COUNT(c.[CustomerID]) < 1000);
```

The TOP clause

The TOP clause is used to limit the number of rows returned by the query. For example, you can either use the TOP keyword to return the first *n* rows or the first *n* percent of rows from a result set. For example, enter and execute the following T-SQL query to return a list of the 10 most expensive products:

```
SELECT TOP (10)
        [ProductID],
        [Name],
        [ProductNumber],
        [ListPrice]
FROM [Production].[Product]
ORDER BY [ListPrice] DESC;
```

The DISTINCT clause

We use the DISTINCT clause to remove duplicates from the result set. For example, to return a distinct list of product names, we run the following query:

```
SELECT DISTINCT
        [Name]
FROM [Production].[Product];
```

Pivoting and unpivoting data

We can use the PIVOT relational operator to swap the specified column values into multiple columns. The UNPIVOT relational operator performs the opposite operation by changing the columns into rows.

The following is the basic syntax of the PIVOT statement:

```
SELECT <non-pivoted column>,
    [first pivoted column] AS <column name>,
    [second pivoted column] AS <column name>,
    ...
    [last pivoted column] AS <column name>
FROM table_source
PIVOT ( aggregate_function ( value_column )
FOR pivot_column
IN ( <column_list>)
) table_alias
```

For example, examine the output of the following query, which returns the count of employees in each group:

```
SELECT p.[BusinessEntityID] , d.[GroupName]
FROM [HumanResources].[Employee] e
INNER JOIN [HumanResources].[EmployeeDepartmentHistory] dhist
ON e.[BusinessEntityID] = dhist.[BusinessEntityID]
AND dhist.[EndDate] IS NULL
INNER JOIN [Person].[Person] p
ON p.[BusinessEntityID] = e.[BusinessEntityID]
INNER JOIN [HumanResources].[Department] d
ON dhist.[DepartmentID] = d.[DepartmentID];
```

The following screenshot shows the output of the preceding query:

	BusinessEntityID	GroupName
1	258	Inventory Management
2	125	Inventory Management
3	186	Manufacturing
4	19	Sales and Marketing
5	173	Manufacturing
6	23	Sales and Marketing
7	9	Research and Development
8	248	Executive General and Administration
9	193	Manufacturing
10	129	Manufacturing
11	38	Manufacturing
12	12	Research and Development
13	155	Manufacturing
14	98	Manufacturing
15	287	Sales and Marketing
16	197	Manufacturing
17	199	Manufacturing
18	286	Sales and Marketing
19	87	Manufacturing
20	208	Manufacturing
21	92	Manufacturing
22	30	Manufacturing
23	276	Sales and Marketing
24	130	Manufacturing

Now, suppose you want to write a query to determine the total number of employees in each group. To accomplish this, you pivot the group column values into columns, along with the count of employees in each group. The following code snippet will help you perform this:

```
SELECT  [Executive General and Administration] , [Inventory
Management] , [Manufacturing] , [Quality Assurance] , [Research
and Development] ,[Sales and Marketing]
FROM (SELECT p.BusinessEntityID , d.[GroupName]
FROM [HumanResources].[Employee] e
INNER JOIN [HumanResources].[EmployeeDepartmentHistory] dhist
ON e.[BusinessEntityID] = dhist.[BusinessEntityID]
AND dhist.[EndDate] IS NULL
INNER JOIN [Person].[Person] p
ON p.[BusinessEntityID] = e.[BusinessEntityID]
INNER JOIN [HumanResources].[Department] d
ON dhist.[DepartmentID] = d.[DepartmentID]
) AS a PIVOT
(COUNT(a.[BusinessEntityID])
FOR [GroupName] IN ([Executive General and Administration],
[Inventory Management], [Manufacturing], [Quality Assurance],
[Research and Development], [Sales and Marketing])) AS b;
```

The preceding query returns information in the format shown in the following screenshot:

	Executive General and Administration	Inventory Management	Manufacturing	Quality Assurance	Research and Development	Sales and Marketing
1	36	19	186	12	15	28

Using the Transact-SQL analytic window functions

SQL Server 2014 supports several analytic functions. With the help of these window analytic functions, we can perform common analyses, such as ranking, percentiles, moving averages, and cumulative sums that can be expressed concisely in a single SELECT statement.

Before the advent of analytic functions, the solution for performing complex analytical tasks was to use self joins, correlated subqueries, temporary tables, or some combination of all three. This solution was inefficient and highly resource intensive. Expressing queries with analytic functions simplifies complex tasks by eliminating programming self joins and correlated subqueries. It also uses fewer temporary tables.

In this section, we will cover all SQL Server 2014 analytic functions.

Ranking functions

We use ranking functions to return the ranking value for the rows within a query result set or partition. The rows in a partition can receive the same ranking value, which depends on the ranking function that is used.

There are four ranking functions, which are listed here:

- ROW_NUMBER: This function assigns a row number to each row in the result set.

- RANK: This function returns the rank value for each row in the result set, but with gaps.

- DENSE_RANK: This function is the same as the RANK function, but also displays the rank value for each row in the result set and without gaps in the sequence.

- NTILE: This function partitions the ranks into a specific number of groups. For example, suppose you have a table with 30 values; you can use NTILE(3) to group the first 10 rows as group 1, the middle 10 rows as group 2, and the last 10 rows as group 3.

We must specify a mandatory OVER clause with sorting functions. The OVER clause determines the partition and order of rows in a result set or partition before applying the ranking functions.

The following is the general syntax of ranking functions:

```
FUNCTION (Argument1,…[n])
OVER ([PARTITION BY value_expression,…[n]) <<Order_by_clause>>)
```

The following query demonstrates the use of ranking functions based on the SalesQuota column:

```
SELECT  [LastName] ,
        [FirstName],
        [SalesQuota],
        ROW_NUMBER() OVER ( ORDER BY
                [SalesQuota]) [ROW_NUMBER],
        RANK() OVER (ORDER BY
                [SalesQuota]) [RANK],
        DENSE_RANK() OVER (ORDER BY
                [SalesQuota]) [DENSE_RANK],
        NTILE(10) OVER (ORDER BY
                [SalesQuota]) AS [NTILE]
FROM    [Sales].[vSalesPerson] ;
```

The preceding code returns the information shown in the following screenshot:

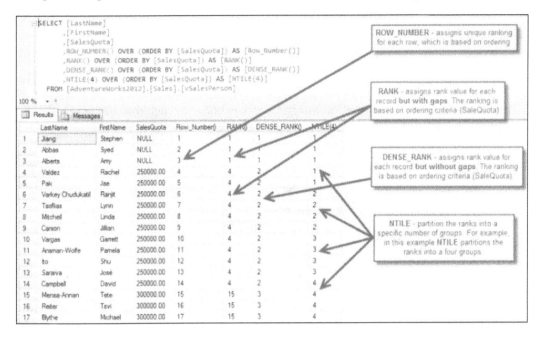

We can use the optional PARTITION BY clause, which partitions the rows based on the value expression and then ranks the rows in the order specified. For example, enter and execute the following T-SQL query to partition the result set by the CountryRegionName column:

```
SELECT    [LastName],
          [FirstName],
          [SalesQuota],
          [CountryRegionName],
          ROW_NUMBER() OVER
              (PARTITION BY [CountryRegionName]
              ORDER BY [SalesQuota]) [ROW_NUMBER],
          RANK() OVER
              (PARTITION BY [CountryRegionName]
              ORDER BY [SalesQuota]) [RANK],
          DENSE_RANK() OVER
              (PARTITION BY [CountryRegionName]
              ORDER BY [SalesQuota]) [DENSE_RANK],
          NTILE(4) OVER
              (PARTITION BY [CountryRegionName]
              ORDER BY [SalesQuota]) AS [NTILE]
FROM      [Sales].[vSalesPerson];
```

The preceding code returns the result set shown in the following screenshot:

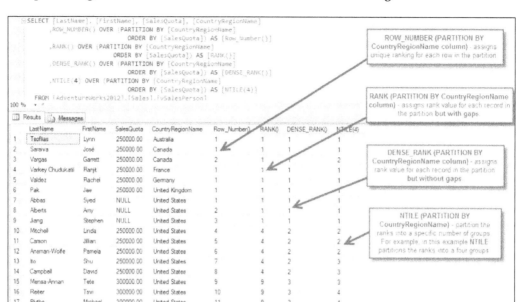

PERCENT RANK

The purpose of the PERCENT_RANK function is to calculate the relative position of each row in a query result set or within a partition. SQL Server uses the following formula to calculate the value of the PERCENT_RANK column:

```
(rank()-1) / (total rows in a query result set or partition-1)
```

As an example, enter and execute the following T-SQL query, which uses the PERCENT_RANK function to compute the rank of a salesperson's sales quota within a country as a percentage. The PARTITION BY clause is specified for the partitioning of the rows in the result set by country region name, and the ORDER BY clause sorts the rows in each partition.

```
SELECT   [LastName] ,
         [FirstName] ,
         [SalesQuota] ,
         [CountryRegionName] ,
         PERCENT_RANK() OVER
(PARTITION BY [CountryRegionName]
ORDER BY [SalesQuota]) [PERCENT_RANK]
FROM     [Sales].[vSalesPerson]
WHERE    [SalesQuota] IS NOT NULL;
```

The preceding code returns the result set shown in the following screenshot:

	LastName	FirstName	SalesQuota	CountryRegionName	PERCENT_RANK
1	Tsoflias	Lynn	250000.00	Australia	0
2	Vargas	Garrett	250000.00	Canada	0
3	Saraiva	José	250000.00	Canada	0
4	Varkey Chudukatil	Ranjit	250000.00	France	0
5	Valdez	Rachel	250000.00	Germany	0
6	Pak	Jae	250000.00	United Kingdom	0
7	Campbell	David	250000.00	United States	0
8	Ansman-Wolfe	Pamela	250000.00	United States	0
9	Ito	Shu	250000.00	United States	0
10	Mitchell	Linda	250000.00	United States	0
11	Carson	Jillian	250000.00	United States	0
12	Reiter	Tsvi	300000.00	United States	0.714285714285714
13	Mensa-Annan	Tete	300000.00	United States	0.714285714285714
14	Blythe	Michael	300000.00	United States	0.714285714285714

CUME_DIST

We use the CUME_DIST function to evaluate the cumulative distribution value for a group of values in a given result set or partition. SQL Server uses the following formula to calculate the value of the CUME_DIST column:

```
(Values less than or equal to the current value in the group)
/ (total row in a query result set or partition)
```

For example, the following query uses the CUME_DIST function to calculate the sales quota percentile for each salesperson within a particular country. The value returned by the CUME_DIST function represents the percentage of salespeople in the same country who have a sales quota that is less than or equal to that of the salesperson we have chosen to analyze.

```
SELECT   [LastName] ,
         [FirstName] ,
         [SalesQuota] ,
         [CountryRegionName] ,
         CUME_DIST() OVER
            (PARTITION BY [CountryRegionName]
            ORDER BY [SalesQuota]) [CUME_DIST]
FROM     [Sales].[vSalesPerson]
WHERE    [SalesQuota] IS NOT NULL;
```

The following screenshot shows the results of this query:

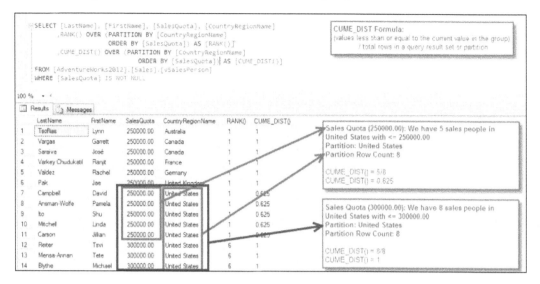

PERCENTILE_CONT and PERCENTILE_DISC

The PERCENTILE_CONT function uses a discrete distribution model to calculate a percentile. The PERCENTILE_CONT function accepts the percentile value (that is, the desired CUME_DIST value) and a sort specification to return the value that would fall into that percentile value. The PERCENTILE_DISC function works in the same way as a PERCENTILE_CONT function because it also returns the smallest value whose percentile is greater than or equal to the given percentile.

Here is the general syntax of PERCENTILE_CONT and PERCENTILE_DISC:

```
PERCENTILE_CONT | PERCENTILE_DISC (numeric_literal)
WITHIN GROUP
(ORDER BY order_by_expression [ASC|DESC])
OVER ([<partition_by_clause>])
```

For example, enter and execute the following T-SQL query, which uses PERCENTILE_CONT and PERCENTILE_DISC to find the median employee salary in each business entity. These functions do not always return the same value because PERCENTILE_CONT interpolates the correct value, which may not exist in the data set, while PERCENTILE_DISC always gives an actual value of the set.

```
SELECT TOP 15
        [BusinessEntityID],
        [Rate],
```

```
       PERCENTILE_CONT(0.5)
           WITHIN GROUP
(ORDER BY [Rate]) OVER
(PARTITION BY [BusinessEntityID]) [PERCENTILE_CONT],
       PERCENTILE_DISC(0.5)
           WITHIN GROUP
(ORDER BY [Rate]) OVER
(PARTITION BY [BusinessEntityID]) [PERCENTILE_DISC]
FROM    [HumanResources].[EmployeePayHistory];
```

Examine the following output of this query:

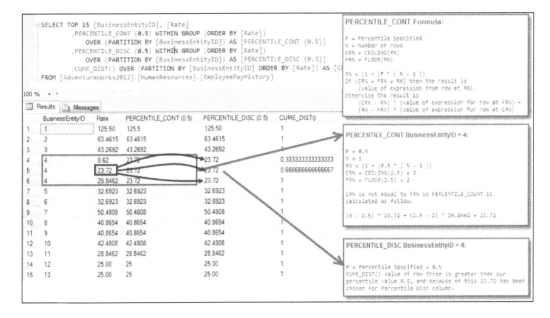

LEAD and LAG

The LEAD function provides access to the row following the current row. The LAG function is the opposite of LEAD, which provides access to the previous row instead of the row following the current row. Here is the general syntax:

```
LAG (scalar_expression [,offset] [,default])
OVER ([partition_by_clause] order_by_clause)
```

The following example uses the LEAD and LAG functions to compare year-to-date sales among the employees, partitioned by sales territory, that are included in the AdventureWorks2012 database:

```
SELECT  [FirstName],
        [TerritoryGroup],
        [SalesYTD],
        LEAD([SalesYTD])
        OVER (PARTITION BY [TerritoryGroup]
        ORDER BY [SalesYTD]) [Next_Lower_SalesYTD(LEAD)],
        LAG([SalesYTD])
        OVER (PARTITION BY [TerritoryGroup]
        ORDER BY [SalesYTD]) [Prev_Higer_SalesYTD(LAG)]
FROM    [Sales].[vSalesPerson]
WHERE   [TerritoryGroup] IS NOT NULL;
```

The preceding query returns the result shown in the following screenshot:

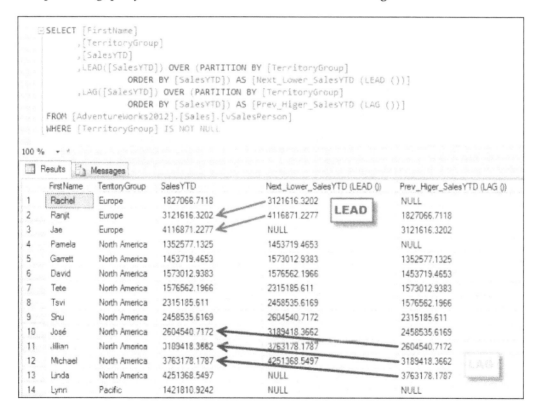

FIRST_VALUE and LAST_VALUE

We use the FIRST_VALUE function to return the first value in the result set or partition. We use the LAST_VALUE function to return the last value in the result set or partition. If the last value in the set is NULL, the LAST_VALUE function returns NULL unless we specify IGNORE NULLS.

When not specified, the row's range clause defaults to RANGE BETWEEN UNBOUNDED PRECEDING AND CURRENT ROW, which sometimes returns an unexpected value. This is because the last value in the window is fixed. For proper results, specify the row range as either RANGE BETWEEN UNBOUNDED PRECEDING AND UNBOUNDED FOLLOWING or RANGE BETWEEN CURRENT ROW AND UNBOUNDED FOLLOWING.

For example, the following query uses the FIRST_VALUE and LAST_VALUE functions to return the highest and lowest year-to-date sales figures for each sales territory:

```
SELECT DISTINCT
[TerritoryGroup] ,
FIRST_VALUE([SalesYTD])
OVER (PARTITION BY [TerritoryGroup] ORDER BY [SalesYTD]
ROWS BETWEEN UNBOUNDED PRECEDING AND CURRENT ROW)
AS [Highest_SalesYTD (FIRST_VALUE)] ,
LAST_VALUE([SalesYTD])
OVER (PARTITION BY [TerritoryGroup]
ORDER BY [SalesYTD]
RANGE BETWEEN CURRENT ROW AND UNBOUNDED FOLLOWING )
AS [Lowest_SalesYTD (FIRST_VALUE)]
FROM [Sales].[vSalesPerson]
WHERE [TerritoryGroup] IS NOT NULL;
```

The following screenshot shows the output of the preceding query:

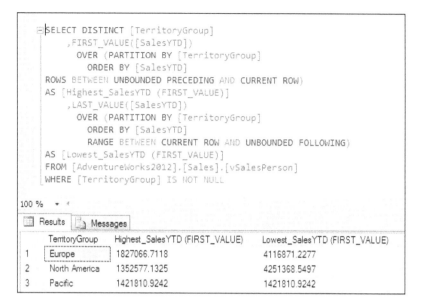

Summary

In this chapter, you learned the basic syntax of the SELECT statement and how it can be used to query data from SQL Server database tables. You learned about the different categories of built-in T-SQL functions and used them in your queries. You learned the different techniques to combine data from multiple tables. You also learned how to organize the data and how to generate the summary data by grouping data or pivoting data. You also understood the purpose of the CTE. We then went through the purpose of window analytic functions and how to use them to quickly solve complex analytical tasks.

4
Data Modification with SQL Server Transact-SQL Statements

In the previous chapter, you learned how to query data stored in the SQL Server database tables. In this chapter, you will learn how to insert, update, and delete data in tables using Transact-SQL **Data Manipulation Language** (**DML**) statements. You will also learn how you can use Transact-SQL MERGE statements to perform multiple DML operations against a specified target table based on the results of join conditions with a source table. In the final section of this chapter, you will use Transact-SQL TRUNCATE TABLE statements to remove all data from a table, and use Transact-SQL SELECT INTO statements to create a table and (optionally) populate it with rows from a query.

In this chapter, we'll cover the following topics:

- Inserting data into SQL Server database tables
- Updating data in SQL Server database tables
- Deleting data from SQL Server database tables
- Using Transact-SQL MERGE statements to perform multiple DML operations using a single code block
- Using TRUNCATE TABLE statements
- Using SELECT INTO statements

Inserting data into SQL Server database tables

In SQL Server, you use the INSERT statement to add one new row or multiple new rows to an existing table. You can use the INSERT statement to insert data into a particular column, all columns, and IDENTITY columns.

To execute INSERT statements, a user must have at least the INSERT permission assigned on the target table.

The following is the basic syntax for INSERT statements:

```
[WITH <common_table_expression> [,...n]]
INSERT [TOP (expression) [PERCENT]
[INTO]
table_name | view_name | rowset function | common_table_expression
[WITH table_hints ]
<output_clause>
[(column_list)]
{VALUES (values_list) | select_statement | DEFAULT |
execute_statement | dml_table_source
NULL
} | DEFAULT VALUES
```

The column_list parameter specifies a list of one or more columns in which you are inserting data. The column_list parameter is optional when you are providing a value for each column in the table, and the values appear in the exact order in which the columns are defined. If a column does not appear, then SQL Server must generate a value for that column. SQL Server can automatically provide values for IDENTITY columns, columns with the timestamp data type, columns with a default value, and nullable columns.

Although the column_list parameters are optional for the SELECT and INSERT statements, it is always a good idea to provide a full-column list for these statements. This is because if the full-column list is not specified, SQL Server resolves full-column lists whenever the SELECT and INSERT statements execute. Moreover, the SELECT or INSERT statement may generate an error if the underlying table schema changes.

The other arguments of the INSERT statement are explained as follows:

- WITH: This keyword specifies the **common table expression** (**CTE**) that you can reference in your INSERT statement.

- TOP: Specify this keyword if you want to insert a specific number or percent of rows from the top of the query result.

- table_name | view_name | rowset function | common_table_expression: This specifies the name of the table, view, rowset function, or CTE in which you want to insert data.

- WITH table_hints: You use this keyword to specify one or more table hints for the target table.

- output_clause: You use this keyword to identify the rows affected by the INSERT statement.

- VALUES: This keyword specifies the data values to be inserted. You must provide a value for each column specified in the column_list parameter. Otherwise, you must provide a value for each column in the table.

- value_list: Values can be constants, variables, or expressions. If an expression is used, it cannot contain SELECT or EXECUTE. You can specify DEFAULT to have a column use its default value, or use NULL to set a column value to NULL.

- select_statement: If a SELECT statement is used, each result set must be compatible with the table columns or the column list.

- DEFAULT: When you use DEFAULT, the SQL Server Database Engine inserts the default value, or (if the column allows NULL) a NULL value is inserted to the column.

- execute_statement: This can be any valid EXECUTE statement that returns data with a SELECT statement. You can also use EXECUTE to execute a stored procedure that returns data with a SELECT statement. If an EXECUTE statement is used, each result set must be compatible with the columns of the table or the column list.

- dml_table_source: This can be any valid DML statement that returns the affected rows in an OUTPUT clause.

- DEFAULT_VALUE: When you use DEFAULT_VALUE, SQL Server inserts a new row with the default values defined for each column.

The INSERT examples

This section describes the various forms of INSERT statements used to insert data into a SQL Server database table. To illustrate the INSERT statement, create the dbo.CustomProducts table within the AdventureWorks2012 database. Here is the code to create this table:

```
USE [AdventureWorks2012];
GO
IF OBJECT_ID(N'dbo.CustomProducts', N'U') IS NOT NULL
    DROP TABLE [dbo].[CustomProducts];
GO

CREATE TABLE [dbo].[CustomProducts]
    (
       [ProductID] [int] IDENTITY(1, 1)
                       NOT NULL,
       [ProductName] [varchar](50) NULL
               DEFAULT ('Anonymous'),
       [ProductCategory] [varchar](50) NULL
               DEFAULT ('Anonymous'),
       [ListPrice] [money] NOT NULL
               DEFAULT (1.0),
       [ListPriceCurrency] VARCHAR(30)
               DEFAULT ('US Dollar'),
       [SellStartDate] [datetime] NOT NULL
               DEFAULT CURRENT_TIMESTAMP,
       [SellEndDate] [datetime] NULL
    )
ON [PRIMARY];
GO
```

Example 1 – insert a single row into a SQL Server database table

In **Object Explorer**, enter and execute the following INSERT statement to add a single row to the dbo.CustomProducts table:

```
INSERT  INTO [dbo].[CustomProducts]
          ([ProductName],
           [ProductCategory],
           [ListPrice],
           [ListPriceCurrency],
           [SellStartDate],
```

```
            [SellEndDate]
            )
VALUES    (N'iPhone 5s',
          N'Gadget',
          25,
          N'GB',
          CURRENT_TIMESTAMP,
          DEFAULT
          );
GO
```

Execute the following code to show the new row:

```
USE [AdventureWorks2012];
GO

SELECT * FROM [dbo].[CustomProducts];
GO
```

The following screenshot shows the new row:

	ProductID	ProductName	ProductCategory	ListPrice	ListPriceCurrency	SellStartDate	SellEndDate
1	1	iPhone 5s	Gadget	549.00	GB	2014-04-27 14:43:27.613	NULL

You can also use the INSERT statement to insert multiple rows in a table. This is done by providing a comma-delimited list of values for each row in the VALUE clause. For example, enter and execute the following T-SQL code to add three rows to the dbo.CustomProducts table:

```
USE [AdventureWorks2012];
GO

INSERT   INTO [dbo].[CustomProducts]
        ( [ProductName], [ProductCategory], [ListPrice],
        [ListPriceCurrency],
        [SellStartDate], [SellEndDate] )
VALUES   (N'Samsung Galaxy S5', N'Gadget', 426, N'GB',
CURRENT_TIMESTAMP, DEFAULT )
        ,(N'HTC One (M8)', N'Gadget', 609, N'USD',
CURRENT_TIMESTAMP, DEFAULT ),
        (N'Nokia Lumia 1520', N'Gadget', 529, N'USD',
CURRENT_TIMESTAMP,DEFAULT );
GO
```

You can query the `dbo.CustomProducts` table again to verify the new rows inserted with the multirow `INSERT` statement. The result will be similar to the one shown in the following screenshot:

	ProductID	ProductName	ProductCategory	ListPrice	ListPriceCurrency	SellStartDate	SellEndDate
1	1	iPhone 5s	Gadget	549.00	GB	2014-04-27 14:43:27.613	NULL
2	2	Samsung Galaxy S5	Gadget	426.00	GB	2014-04-27 14:55:17.860	NULL
3	3	HTC One (M8)	Gadget	609.00	USD	2014-04-27 14:55:17.860	NULL
4	4	Nokia Lumia 1520	Gadget	529.00	USD	2014-04-27 14:55:17.860	NULL

Example 2 – INSERT with the SELECT statement

You can also use the `SELECT` statement within an `INSERT` statement to insert data rows that already exist in the same table, other tables, or even the tables of a different database. For example, the following `INSERT` statement uses the `SELECT` statement to insert rows in the `dbo.CustomProducts` table:

```
USE [AdventureWorks2012];
GO

INSERT  INTO [dbo].[CustomProducts]
        ( [ProductName], [ProductCategory], [ListPrice],
          [ListPriceCurrency],
          [SellStartDate], [SellEndDate])
SELECT  p.[Name],
        pc.[Name],
        [ListPrice],
        N'USD',
        [SellStartDate],
        [SellEndDate]
FROM    [Production].[Product] p
        INNER JOIN [Production].[ProductCategory] pc
        ON p.[ProductSubcategoryID] = PC.ProductCategoryID;
GO
```

Example 3 – INSERT with the EXEC statement

As mentioned in the preceding section, you can insert data into a table from the results of the `EXECUTE` statement. For example, enter and execute the following T-SQL code to insert the `xp_msver` stored procedure output into a temporary table:

```
USE [AdventureWorks2012];
GO

IF OBJECT_ID(N'Tempdb..#xp_msver') IS NOT NULL
```

```
DROP TABLE #xp_msver
GO

CREATE TABLE #xp_msver
    (
        [idx] [int] NULL,
        [c_name] [varchar](100) NULL,
        [int_val] [float] NULL,
        [c_val] [varchar](128) NULL
    )

INSERT  INTO #xp_msver
EXEC ('[master]..[xp_msver]');
GO
```

Example 4 – explicitly inserting data into the IDENTITY column

By default, the SQL Server Database Engine generates the values for the IDENTITY columns. You cannot explicitly insert values into the IDENTITY property columns, unless you specify the IDENTITY_INSERT option. For example, SQL Server generates the following error when you attempt to insert a value into the IDENTITY property column:

```
Msg 544, Level 16, State 1, Line 27
Cannot insert explicit value for identity column in table
'CustomProducts' when IDENTITY_INSERT is set to OFF.
```

To explicitly insert values into the IDENTITY property column, use the IDENTITY_INSERT option. The basic syntax for this command is as follows:

```
SET IDENTITY_INSERT [database.[owner.]]table ON|OFF
```

For example, the following T-SQL code uses the IDENTITY_INSERT option and inserts an explicit value into the ProductID column:

```
USE [AdventureWorks2012];
GO

SET IDENTITY_INSERT [dbo].[CustomProducts] ON;

INSERT  INTO [dbo].[CustomProducts]
        ( [ProductID] ,
          [ProductName] ,
          [ProductCategory] ,
```

```
                 [ListPrice] ,
                 [ListPriceCurrency] ,
                 [SellStartDate] ,
                 [SellEndDate]
             )
   VALUES  ( 110 ,
                 N'Samsung Galaxy S4',
                 N'Gadget',
                 200,
                 N'GB',
                 CURRENT_TIMESTAMP,
                 DEFAULT
             );

   SET IDENTITY_INSERT [dbo].[CustomProducts] OFF;
   GO
```

Updating data in SQL Server database tables

You use the UPDATE statement to modify an existing table data.

To execute the UPDATE statement, a user must have at least an UPDATE permission assigned on the target table.

The following is the basic syntax for the UPDATE statement:

```
[WITH <common_table_expression> [, ...n]]
UPDATE
[TOP (expression) [PERCENT]]
table_name | view_name | rowset_function | common_table_expression
[WITH table_hint]
SET column_name = {expression | DEFAULT | NULL} [ ,...n ]
<outputclause>
FROM < table_name | view_name | common_table_expression>
WHERE <search_condition>
```

The following are the arguments of the UPDATE statement:

- WITH: This keyword specifies the CTE that you can reference in your UPDATE statement
- TOP: You specify this keyword to only update a specific number or percent of rows from the top of the query

- `table_name | view_name | rowset function | common_table_expression`: This specifies the name of the table, view, rowset function, or CTE that contains the data to be updated

- `SET`: This specifies the name of the column or columns to be updated

- `FROM`: This keyword specifies the name of the table, view, or CTE from which you are taking the data

- `WHERE`: This keyword specifies the search condition to identify which records are to be updated

- `WITH table_hints`: You use this keyword to specify one or more table hints for the destination table

- `output_clause`: You use this to identify the rows affected by the `UPDATE` statement

The UPDATE statement examples

This section describes the basic forms of the `UPDATE` statement.

Example 1 – updating a single row

The following `UPDATE` statement updates the list price of a single product in the `Production.Product` table:

```
USE [AdventureWorks2012];
GO

UPDATE [Production].[Product]
SET [ListPrice] = 1670
WHERE [ProductID] = 13;
GO
```

Example 2 – updating multiple rows

Suppose you want to increase the list price by 25 percent only for products whose list price is less than $1,000. To accomplish this, you need to run the following `UPDATE` statement in the SSMS 2014 Query Editor:

```
USE [AdventureWorks2012];
GO

UPDATE [Production].[Product]
SET [ListPrice] = [ListPrice] + ([ListPrice] * 0.25)
WHERE [ListPrice] < 1000;
GO
```

Another example, the following UPDATE statement, updates the list price to $200 for products whose current price list is $0.0:

```
USE [AdventureWorks2012];
GO

UPDATE [Production].[Product]
SET [ListPrice] = 200.0
WHERE [ListPrice] = 0.0;
GO
```

Deleting data from SQL Server database tables

You use the DELETE statement to delete unwanted data from SQL Server database tables.

To execute the DELETE statement, the user must at least have the DELETE permission assigned on the target table.

The basic syntax for a DELETE statement is as follows:

```
[WITH <common_table_expression> [,...n]]
DELETE
[TOP (expression) [percent]]
[FROM] table_name | view_name | rowset_function
[WITH table_hint]
<outputclause>
[FROM table_source]
WHERE search_conditions
```

The following are the arguments of a DELETE statement:

- WITH: This keyword specifies the CTE that you can reference in your DELETE statement
- TOP: Specify this keyword to only delete a specific number or percent of rows from the top of the query
- table_name | view_name | rowset function | common_table_expression: This specifies the name of the table, view, rowset function, or CTE containing the data that you want to delete
- FROM: This keyword specifies the name of the table, view, or CTE from which you are deleting the data

- `WHERE`: This keyword specifies the search condition to identify which records you want to delete
- `WITH table_hints`: You use this keyword to specify one or more table hints for the destination table
- `output_clause`: You use this to identify the rows affected by a `DELETE` statement

The DELETE statement examples

The following are the two examples of the `DELETE` statement.

Example 1 – deleting a single row

The following `DELETE` statement deletes all rows from the `dbo.CustomProducts` table in which the `ProductCategory` column value is `Components`:

```
USE [AdventureWorks2012];
GO

DELETE FROM [dbo].[CustomProducts]
WHERE [ProductCategory] = N'Components';
GO
```

Example 2 – deleting all rows

Execute the following `DELETE` statement to delete all rows from the `dbo.CustomProducts` table:

```
USE [AdventureWorks2012];
GO

DELETE FROM [dbo].[CustomProducts];
GO
```

Using the MERGE statement

In SQL Server, you can perform multiple DML operations in a single code block using the `MERGE` statement. The `MERGE` statement is a powerful Transact-SQL language feature that allows you to join a source table with a target table, and then perform multiple DML operations against the specified target table, based on the results of the `MERGE` statement join conditions. By using a `MERGE` statement, you can improve the performance of OLTP applications, since the data is processed only once.

To execute a MERGE statement, a user must at least have a SELECT permission assigned on the source table and INSERT, UPDATE, and DELETE permissions assigned on the target table.

The basic syntax for the MERGE statement is as follows:

```
[ WITH <common_table_expression> [,...n] ]
MERGE
    [ TOP ( expression ) [ PERCENT ] ]
    [ INTO ] <target_table> [ WITH ( <merge_hint> ) ]
    USING <source_table>
    ON <merge_search_condition>
    [ WHEN MATCHED [ AND <search_condition> ]
        THEN <merge_matched> ] [ ...n ]
    [ WHEN NOT MATCHED [ BY TARGET ] [ AND <search_condition> ]
        THEN <merge_not_matched> ]
    [ WHEN NOT MATCHED BY SOURCE [ AND <search_condition> ]
        THEN <merge_matched> ] [ ...n ]
    [ <output_clause> ]
    [ OPTION ( <query_hint> [ ,...n ] ) ] ;
```

The following are the arguments of the MERGE statement:

- WITH: This keyword specifies the CTE that you can reference in your MERGE statement.

- TOP: You use this keyword only to perform DML operations on a specific number or percent of rows from the top of the joined rows.

- target_table: This specifies the name of the target table against which the source table rows are matched.

- USING <source_table>: This specifies the name of the source table that is matched with the target table.

- ON: This keyword specifies the MERGE statement join conditions to identify which records should be affected.

- WHEN MATCHED: These keywords specify all rows that exist in both the source and target tables. Based on these matching rows, update or delete data in the target table.

- WHEN NOT MATCHED [BY TARGET]: These keywords specify all rows in the source table that do not exist in the target table. Based on the results of the <merge_search_condition> condition, you insert the data into the target table. You can only have one WHEN NOT MATCHED clause in the MERGE statement.

- `WHEN NOT MATCHED BY SOURCE`: These keywords specifies all rows in the target table that do not exist in the source table. Based on the results of the `<merge_search_condition>` condition, you either update or delete data in the target table.

- `output_clause`: You use this to identify the rows affected by the `MERGE` statement.

- `OPTION (<query_hint> [ ,...n ])`: You use this keyword to specify one or more optimizer query hints.

The MERGE statement examples

To illustrate the `MERGE` statement, consider the following two tables:

- `dbo.Spices`: This database contains information about the spices that the company is currently selling

- `dbo.SpicesNew`: This database contains information about the spices that the company will sell in the future

The following T-SQL code creates and populates these two tables:

```
USE [AdventureWorks2012];
GO

IF OBJECT_ID(N'dbo.Spices', N'U') IS NOT NULL
    DROP TABLE [dbo].[Spices];
GO
CREATE TABLE [dbo].[Spices]
    (
       [SpiceID] [int] PRIMARY KEY,
       [SpiceMixName] [nvarchar](64),
       [Supplier] [nvarchar](50)
    );

IF OBJECT_ID(N'dbo.Spices_New', N'U') IS NOT NULL
    DROP TABLE [dbo].[Spices_New];
GO
CREATE TABLE [dbo].[Spices_New]
    (
       [SpiceID] [int] PRIMARY KEY,
       [SpiceMixName] [nvarchar](64),
       [Supplier] [nvarchar](50)
    );
```

```
INSERT   INTO [dbo].[Spices]
VALUES  ( 1, N'Five-spice powder', N'Go it!' )
    ,       ( 2, N'Curry powder', N'East-end Spices' )
    ,       ( 3, N'Garam masala', N'All Spices' )
    ,       ( 4, N'Harissa', N'More Places For Stuff' )
    ,       ( 5, N'Shichimi togarashI', N'World-wide Supply' )
    ,       ( 6, N'Mixed spice', N'UK Spices' )
    ,       ( 7, N'Old Bay Seasoning', N'US Mixed Spices' )
    ,       ( 8, N'Jerk spice', N'Quality Spices' );

INSERT   INTO [dbo].[Spices_New]
VALUES  ( 1, N'Advieh', N'Outlander Spices' )
    ,       ( 2, N'Baharat', N'Spice Source' )
    ,       ( 3, N'Berbere', N'International Supply' )
    ,       ( 4, N'Bumbu', N'Natural Farms' )
    ,       ( 5, N'Chaat masala', N'Sells All' )
    ,       ( 6, N'Chili powder', N'Jo''s Stuff' )
    ,       ( 9, N'Curry powder', N'VJC Processing' );

SELECT * FROM [dbo].[Spices];
SELECT * FROM [dbo].[Spices_New];
GO
```

Now, suppose you want to synchronize the dbo.Spices target table with the dbo.Spices_New source table. Here is the criterion for this task:

- Spices that exist in both the dbo.Spices_New source table and the dbo.Spices target table are updated in the dbo.Spices target table with new names

- Any spices in the dbo.Spices_New source table that do not exist in the dbo.Spices target table are inserted into the dbo.Spices table target table

- Any spices in the dbo.Spices target table that do not exist in the dbo.Spices_New source table must be deleted from the dbo.Spices target table

Without the MERGE statement, one has to write multiple DML statements to accomplish this task. Moreover, for each DML operation, SQL Server processes the data separately, resulting in more time taken to complete each task. However, with the MERGE statement, you can perform this task in a single statement. Here is the MERGE statement to perform this task:

```
USE [AdventureWorks2012];
GO

MERGE [dbo].[Spices] AS [SourceTbl]
USING [dbo].[Spices_New] AS [TargetTbl]
```

```
ON ( SourceTbl.[SpiceID] = TargetTbl.[SpiceID] )
WHEN MATCHED AND SourceTbl.[SpiceMixName] <>
TargetTbl.[SpiceMixName]
    OR SourceTbl.[Supplier] <> TargetTbl.[Supplier] THEN
    UPDATE SET SourceTbl.[SpiceMixName] = TargetTbl.[SpiceMixName]
,
            SourceTbl.[Supplier] = TargetTbl.[Supplier]
WHEN NOT MATCHED THEN
    INSERT ( [SpiceID] ,
            [SpiceMixName] ,
            [Supplier]
        )
    VALUES ( TargetTbl.[SpiceID] ,
            TargetTbl.[SpiceMixName] ,
            TargetTbl.[Supplier]
        )
WHEN NOT MATCHED BY SOURCE THEN
    DELETE
OUTPUT
    $action ,
    INSERTED.* ,
    DELETED.*;
GO
```

The following screenshot shows the rows affected by this MERGE statement:

	$action	SpiceID	SpiceMixName	Supplier	SpiceID	SpiceMixName	Supplier
1	UPDATE	1	Advieh	Outlander Spices	1	Five-spice powder	Go it!
2	UPDATE	2	Baharat	Spice Source	2	Curry powder	East-end Spices
3	UPDATE	3	Berbere	International S...	3	Garam masala	All Spices
4	UPDATE	4	Bumbu	Natural Farms	4	Harissa	More Places F...
5	UPDATE	5	Chaat masala	Sells All	5	Shichimi togarashl	World-wide Su...
6	UPDATE	6	Chili powder	Jo's Stuff	6	Mixed spice	UK Spices
7	DELETE	NULL	NULL	NULL	7	Old Bay Seasoni...	US Mixed Spi...
8	DELETE	NULL	NULL	NULL	8	Jerk spice	Quality Spices
9	INSERT	9	Curry powder	VJC Processing	NULL	NULL	NULL

The TRUNCATE TABLE statement

The TRUNCATE TABLE statement is another way to delete all rows from a table. Unlike the DELETE statement, SQL Server does not log individual row deletion in a transaction log. Therefore, this operation is not recoverable because when you run the TRUNCATE TABLE statement, SQL Server just logs page deallocations that occur as a result of this operation. The TRUNCATE TABLE statement is much faster when compared to the DELETE statement, with no WHERE clause, because it uses fewer system and database transaction log resources.

You cannot use the TRUNCATE TABLE statement on tables that are referenced by a foreign key constraint, included in an indexed view, or published for transactional or merge replication. In such a situation, you are required to use the DELETE statement without a WHERE clause to remove all rows.

 The TRUNCATE TABLE statement does reset identity value to its seed value, while the DELETE statement does not reset identity value. So, use TRUNCATE TABLE if you also want to reset the identity value to its seed value.

To execute the TRUNCATE TABLE statement, the user must have at least an ALTER permission assigned on the target table. The syntax for this command is as follows:

```
TRUNCATE TABLE [[database.]owner.]table_name
```

The following is the example of the TRUNCATE TABLE statement, which will delete all records from a dbo.CustomProduct table:

```
USE [AdventureWorks2012];
GO

TRUNCATE TABLE [dbo].[CustomProducts];
GO
```

The SELECT INTO statement

The SELECT INTO statement is another way to insert data into SQL Server tables. When you use SELECT INTO, SQL Server creates a new table with the specified name in the default filegroup and then inserts the rows from a SELECT query in the newly created table. This new table is based on the columns you specify in the SELECT list, and it must be unique within a database.

The SELECT...INTO statement has been enhanced in SQL Server 2014, and it can now operate in parallel. The parallel insert functionality of SELECT...INTO requires database compatibility level 110 or higher.

To execute the SELECT...INTO statement, a user must have at least the SELECT permission assigned on the target table and the CREATE TABLE permission assigned on the target database. The following is the basic syntax for a SELECT INTO clause:

```
SELECT [ALL|DISTINCT] select_list
[INTO[[database.]owner.]table_name]
FROM[[[database.]owner.]table_name|view_name|UDF]
[WHERE search_conditions]
[GROUP BY aggregate_free_expression]
[HAVING search_conditions]
[ORDER BY table_or_view_and_column]
[OPTION (query_hint)]
```

For example, the following T-SQL code uses the SELECT INTO statement to create a backup copy of the Production.Product table:

```
USE [AdventureWorks2012];
GO

SELECT *
INTO [Production].[Product_Backup]
FROM [Production].[Product];
GO
```

Summary

The SQL Server Transact-SQL language has a set of DML statements that you can use to manipulate table data. In this chapter, you learned how to add data to a table using the INSERT statement, how to delete the data using the DELETE statement, and how to update existing data using the UPDATE statement. You learned about the MERGE statement and how you can use it to avoid multiple INSERT, UPDATE, and DELETE DML statements. You also learned how to use the TRUNCATE TABLE and SELECT...INTO statements.

5

Understanding Advanced Database Programming Objects and Error Handling

None of the Transact-SQL code that we have written so far in this book is reusable. SQL Server allows you to create reusable programming objects. The SQL Server reusable programming objects include views, stored procedures, functions, and triggers (based on either DDL or DML). In this chapter, we first take a look at variables. Next, we take a look at control-flow statements. Then we take a look at the design and use of each of the programmable objects in turn. Finally, we learn how to handle errors that occur in the Transact-SQL batches and programmable objects using a TRY...CATCH construct.

After completing this chapter, you will be able to:

- Create and use variables
- Add logic around and within the Transact-SQL statements to control program execution
- Design and create user-defined views
- Design and create user-defined stored procedures
- Design and create user-defined functions
- Design and create triggers
- Handle errors that occur within the Transact-SQL statements and programming objects

Creating and using variables

Like other programming languages, the SQL Server Transact-SQL language also allows temporary storage in the form of variables. Variables are stored in memory and are accessible only from the batch or stored procedure, or the function in which they are declared. There are three types of variables you can create in SQL Server: local variables (based on system or user-defined data types), cursor variables (to store a server-side cursor), and table variables (that is, structured like a user-defined table).

We can declare a variable as a standard variable in Transact-SQL by prefixing it with the @ symbol. We use the DECLARE statement to declare a variable or multiple variables.

Creating a local variable

The basic syntax for creating a local variable is as follows:

```
DECLARE @variable_name [AS] data_type
```

By default, all local variables are initialized as NULL. We can assign a value to a local variable in one of the following three ways:

- By using the SET keyword, which is the preferred method
- By using the SELECT statement
- During the declaration of the variable

For example, the following T-SQL code shows the assignment of values to local variables using these methods:

- By using the SET keyword:
  ```
  --Example of assigning a value to the local variable using the
  --SET keyword.
  DECLARE @var1 [int],
          @var2 [varchar](10);

  SET @var1 = 10
  SET @var2 = N'MyValue1';
  ```

- By using the SELECT statement:
  ```
  --Example of assigning a value to the local variable using the
  --SELECT statement.
  DECLARE @var3 [int],
          @var4 [varchar](10);

  SELECT  @var3 = 20 ,
          @var4 = N'MyValue2';
  ```

- During the declaration of the variable:

```
--Example of assigning a value to the local variable at
--declaration.
DECLARE @var5 [int] = 30,
        @var6 [varchar](10) = N'MyValue3';
GO
```

Creating the cursor variable

SQL Server supports cursor variables primarily to provide backward compatibility with batches, scripts, and programmable objects written for earlier SQL Server versions.

The syntax to create a cursor variable is as follows:

```
DECLARE @variable_name CURSOR
```

The following is an example of creating a cursor variable:

```
DECLARE @cur_variable1 CURSOR;
```

Creating the table variable

Table variables behave in the same manner as local variables. A table variable stores the data in the form of a table. They are suitable for smaller data sets (typically less than 1,000 rows). The basic syntax for creating a table variable is as follows:

```
DECLARE @table_variable_name [AS] table
(
[(column_definition) [,...n])]
)
```

The following is a basic example of creating a table variable:

```
DECLARE @Table1 TABLE
    (
      COL1 [int],
      COL2 [varchar](30)
    );
```

As you can see in the previous example, the columns of table variables are defined in the same way as you define columns when creating an actual table. Table variables do not support FOREIGN KEY constraints. Moreover, prior to SQL Server 2014, the only way to create indexes on table variables was by defining the PRIMARY KEY or UNIQUE KEY constraint on the table variable columns. However, SQL Server 2014 Database Engine supports non-unique clustered and non-clustered indexes for table variables. We can define indexes on table variables using new inline index specification syntax. The following is an example of inline index creation on a table variable:

```
DECLARE @Table2 TABLE (
COL1 [int],
COL2 [varchar](30),
COL3 [datetime],
INDEX [ixc_col3] CLUSTERED (col3)
WITH (FILLFACTOR=80),
INDEX [ixnc_col1_col2] NONCLUSTERED (col1, col2)
WITH (FILLFACTOR=80)
);
GO
```

Control-of-flow keywords

Control-of-flow keywords help SQL Server determine when and how Transact-SQL statements should execute. With these keywords, you can add logic around and within Transact-SQL statements to control program execution. Control-of-flow keywords add greater flexibility in OLTP application design and help you write clever code. Control-of-flow keywords include BEGIN...END, IF...ELSE, CASE, WHILE, BREAK, CONTINUE, RETURN, GOTO, and WAITFOR.

BEGIN...END keywords

The BEGIN...END keywords identify a code block. We typically use them to group Transact-SQL statements. The BEGIN...END blocks can be nested. We also use BEGIN...END statements to identify a code block in an IF...ELSE clause, WHILE loop, and CASE element. The following is the basic syntax for the BEGIN...END keyword block:

```
BEGIN
    {
    sql_statement | statement_block
    }
END
```

The following is a basic example of BEGIN...END:

```
USE [AdventureWorks2012];
GO

BEGIN
    DECLARE @Today [datetime];
    SET @Today = CURRENT_TIMESTAMP;

    SELECT TOP 100
           *
    FROM    [HumanResources].[vEmployee];

    SELECT  @Today;
END
```

The IF...ELSE expression

The IF...ELSE block is simply used to make processing decisions based on Boolean (true/false) expressions. For example, it tells SQL Server to run a Transact-SQL statement or a set of statements if the Boolean expression specified in the IF clause returns True, or optionally run an alternate Transact-SQL statement or set of statements if the Boolean expression specified in the IF clause returns False.

 A Boolean expression is one that must return True, False, or NULL. SQL Server treats NULL as False.

We can have an IF clause without an ELSE clause; however, an ELSE clause cannot exist without an IF clause. The IF...ELSE statements can be nested, meaning that an IF or ELSE clause can contain another IF...ELSE structure. The basic syntax for the IF...ELSE block follows:

```
IF Boolean_expression { sql_statement | statement_block }
[ ELSE { sql_statement | statement_block } ]
```

When the block of statements is used in an IF...ELSE block, then you must use the BEGIN...END keywords to identify whether the block is in the IF clause or the ELSE clause. Moreover, if you include a SELECT statement in the expression, you must enclose the statement in parentheses. Here is a basic example of an IF...ELSE block:

```
IF ( SELECT DATENAME(dw, CURRENT_TIMESTAMP)
    ) IN ( N'Friday', N'Saturday', N'Sunday' )
    BEGIN
```

```
        SELECT  'Hey, its weekend!!!';
    END;
ELSE
    BEGIN
        SELECT  N'Its weekday!!!';
    END;
```

A CASE statement

We can also use the CASE statement to make decisions based on an expression. The CASE statement is a conceptually simpler way to perform operations similar to IF...ELSE IF...ELSE. The basic syntax for a CASE statement is as follows:

```
CASE input_expression
WHEN test_result THEN statement_block
WHEN test_result THEN statement_block
...
[ELSE statement_block]
END
```

The input_expression parameter is the value that is tested by the WHEN statements. If the input_expression parameter includes a SELECT statement, then you must enclose the SELECT statement in parentheses. The following is a basic example of the CASE statement:

```
SELECT CASE (SELECT DATENAME(dw, CURRENT_TIMESTAMP))
        WHEN N'Friday' THEN N'Hey, Its Friday!!!'
        WHEN N'Saturday' THEN N'Hey, its Saturday!!!'
        WHEN N'Sunday' THEN N'Hey, its Sunday!!!'
        ELSE N'Its weekday!!!'
      END;
```

WHILE, BREAK, and CONTINUE statements

The WHILE statement is a basic looping construct in SQL Server that is based on a Boolean expression. As long as the expression evaluates to true, SQL Server continues to repeat the execution of the specified T-SQL statement or code block. The basic syntax of the WHILE loop is as follows:

```
WHILE Boolean_expression
{ sql_statement | statement_block | BREAK | CONTINUE }
```

The optional keywords BREAK and CONTINUE can be included with the WHILE loop and are used to control the logic inside the loop. When you specify the BREAK keyword with the WHILE loop, it exits the innermost WHILE loop (in nested loops). If in the outer loop, SQL Server exits the WHILE loop and continues with the next statement. On the other hand, when you specify the CONTINUE keyword, SQL Server restarts the loop at the first statement in the block and ignores any statements following the CONTINUE keyword. Here is a basic example of the WHILE loop:

```
DECLARE @counter [int] = 0
WHILE ( @counter < 10 )
    BEGIN
        IF ( @counter < 5 )
            BEGIN
                SELECT  @counter;
                SET @counter = @counter + 1;
                CONTINUE;
            END;
        ELSE
          SET @counter = @counter + 1;
            IF @counter = 7
                BEGIN
                    SELECT  @counter;
                    BREAK;
                END;
    END;
```

RETURN, GOTO, and WAITFOR statements

We use the RETURN keyword to unconditionally end the procedure, batch, or statement block. We use the GOTO keyword to transfer the execution context of the statement from its current point to the specified line in the GOTO label. SQL Server ignores any statements between these. We use the WAITFOR keyword to suspend execution until the specified time of day is reached, or an interval (up to 24 hours) has passed. The time can be supplied as a literal or with a variable.

[The TRY...CATCH construct and the THROW statement are also part of the control-of-flow language keywords. We will cover these control-of-flow keywords later in this chapter.]

Creating and using views

A view is a virtual table whose result set is derived from a query. In reality, a view is simply a SELECT statement that is saved with the name in the database. Views are used just like regular tables without incurring additional cost, unless you are indexing the view. We typically create views based on one or more tables, views, CTEs, table-valued functions, or a combination of them all. We can reference views in Transact-SQL statements in the same way tables are referenced. We can also perform DML operations on views. The typical uses of views include:

- A denormalized presentation of normalized data
- Limiting access to specific columns of the underlying tables
- Creating a reusable set of data
- Restricting users' access to sensitive data

You should avoid using SELECT * in views, because when you do, the columns list is resolved each time you query the view. Moreover, the result set of the view query changes when the underlying table schema changes. A good practice is returning only those columns that are required.

The ORDER BY clause is not valid in views unless used with a TOP clause.

Creating views with Transact-SQL and SSMS 2014

This section describes how to create and manage views using Transact-SQL DDL statements and SSMS 2014.

Creating, altering, and dropping views with Transact-SQL DDL statements

You can create, alter, and drop views with these Transact-SQL DDL statements: CREATE VIEW, ALTER VIEW, and DROP VIEW.

The CREATE VIEW statement

The syntax for the CREATE VIEW statement is very simple and straightforward, as follows:

```
CREATE VIEW [schema.]view_name [(column_list)]
[WITH view_attributes]
```

```
AS select_statement [;]
[WITH CHECK OPTION]
```

The following are the arguments of the CREATE VIEW statement:

- schema: This specifies the name of the schema in which you are creating a view.

- view_name: This specifies the name of the view; it must be unique within the schema.

- column_list: This specifies the name to be used for a column in the view; it is an optional argument unless you have a derived column.

- WITH view_attributes: This is an optional view attribute. The attributes are as follows:

   - ENCRYPTION: This attribute encrypts the text of the CREATE VIEW statement

   - SCHEMABINDING: This attribute binds the view to the underlying table or tables, meaning users cannot modify the underlying table or tables in any way that affects the view definition

   - VIEW_METADATA: This attribute specifies the instance of SQL Server to return the metadata information about the view instead of the underlying base table or tables to the DB-Library, ODBC, and OLE DB **application programming interfaces (APIs)**

- AS select_statement: This is the SELECT statement defining the view.

- WITH CHECK OPTION: This forces the DML statements executed against the view to follow the criteria in the SELECT statement.

Here is an example of the CREATE VIEW statement:

```
USE [AdventureWorks2012];
GO

CREATE VIEW [HumanResources].[vEmployeesWithinCompanyGroup]
AS
SELECT  [Executive General and Administration] , [Inventory
Management] , [Manufacturing] , [Quality Assurance] , [Research
and Development] ,[Sales and Marketing]
FROM (SELECT p.BusinessEntityID , d.[GroupName]
FROM [HumanResources].[Employee] e
INNER JOIN [HumanResources].[EmployeeDepartmentHistory] dhist
ON e.[BusinessEntityID] = dhist.[BusinessEntityID]
AND dhist.[EndDate] IS NULL
INNER JOIN [Person].[Person] p
ON p.[BusinessEntityID] = e.[BusinessEntityID]
```

```
INNER JOIN [HumanResources].[Department] d
ON dhist.[DepartmentID] = d.[DepartmentID]
) AS a PIVOT
(COUNT(a.[BusinessEntityID])
FOR [GroupName] IN ([Executive General and Administration],
[Inventory Management], [Manufacturing], [Quality Assurance],
[Research and Development], [Sales and Marketing])) AS b
GO
```

The ALTER VIEW statement

We use the ALTER VIEW statement to modify the view definition. The ALTER VIEW statement syntax is the same as the CREATE VIEW statement syntax:

```
ALTER VIEW [schema.]view_name [(column_list)]
[WITH view_attributes]
AS select_statement [;]
[WITH CHECK OPTION]
```

The following is an example of the ALTER VIEW statement:

```
USE [AdventureWorks2012];
GO

ALTER VIEW [HumanResources].[vEmployeesWithinCompanyGroup]
AS
SELECT  [Executive General and Administration] , [Inventory
Management] , [Manufacturing] , [Quality Assurance] , [Research
and Development] ,[Sales and Marketing]
FROM (SELECT p.BusinessEntityID , d.[GroupName]
FROM [HumanResources].[Employee] e
INNER JOIN [HumanResources].[EmployeeDepartmentHistory] dhist
ON e.[BusinessEntityID] = dhist.[BusinessEntityID]
AND dhist.[EndDate] IS NULL
INNER JOIN [Person].[Person] p
ON p.[BusinessEntityID] = e.[BusinessEntityID]
INNER JOIN [HumanResources].[Department] d
ON dhist.[DepartmentID] = d.[DepartmentID]
) AS a PIVOT
(COUNT(a.[BusinessEntityID])
FOR [GroupName] IN ([Executive General and Administration],
[Inventory Management], [Manufacturing], [Quality Assurance],
[Research and Development], [Sales and Marketing])) AS b
GO
```

The DROP VIEW statement

We use the DROP VIEW statement to permanently delete a view. The DROP VIEW statement syntax is as follows:

```
DROP VIEW [schema.]view_name
```

The following is an example of the DROP VIEW statement:

```
USE [AdventureWorks2012];
GO

DROP VIEW [HumanResources].[vEmployeesWithinCompanyGroup];
GO
```

Creating, altering, and dropping views with SSMS 2014

You can use the SQL Server 2014 Management Studio GUI to create, alter, and drop views. This section demonstrates the steps to do that.

Creating views with SSMS 2014

The following are the steps to create views with the SQL Server 2014 Management Studio GUI:

1. Open SQL Server 2014 Management Studio.

2. In **Object Explorer**, expand the Databases folder.

3. Expand the database in which you want to create the view.

4. Right-click on the Views folder and select **New View...** from the context menu. The **Add Table** dialog box now opens, as shown in the following screenshot:

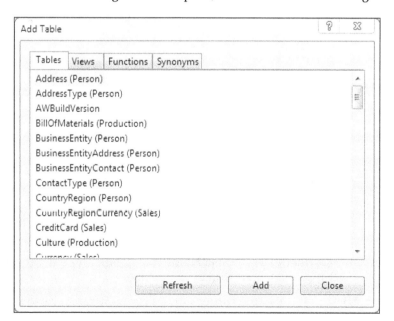

5. Choose all the necessary base objects for your view query and then click on the **Close** button to close the **Add Table** dialog box. The Create View pane is now visible, as shown in the following screenshot:

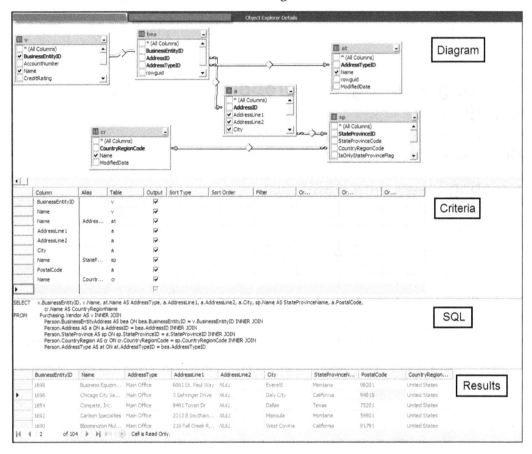

6. You can use the Create View panes to design your views. For example, using the Create View pane, you can perform the following:

    ○ You can use the **Diagram** pane to select the view columns

    ○ You can use the **Criteria** pane to specify the view criteria, such as sort order and filter logic

    ○ You can use the **SQL** pane to directly modify the view query

7. Once satisfied with the changes, click on the save icon in the SSMS 2014 menu bar. This opens the **Choose Name** dialog box. Type in the name of the view and then click on **OK** to save the view.

8. Finally, click on the **X** in the corner of the new view tab to close the view designer GUI.

Altering and dropping views with SSMS 2014

To modify a view in SQL Server 2014 Management Studio, perform the following steps:

1. Expand the Views folder.

2. Right-click on the view and choose **Design** from the context menu.

3. Make the necessary changes to the **Diagram**, **Criteria**, and **SQL** panes.

4. Save the view changes.

> If the view was created using the WITH ENCRYPTION option, you cannot modify it in SSMS. The **Design** option is disabled when you right-click on an encrypted view.

To drop a view in SQL Server 2014 Management Studio, perform the following steps:

1. Expand the Views folder.

2. Right-click on the view and choose **Delete**.

3. Click on **OK** to verify your action.

Indexed views

An indexed view is a persisted view that is stored on disk. The indexed view helps improve performance because, as long as the data in the base objects has not changed, SQL Server can process queries based on views without accessing the base objects. SQL Server Database Engine automatically updates the indexed view indexes if the data in the key columns changes.

> The indexed view feature is available only in the Enterprise edition of SQL Server 2014.

When creating an indexed view, you should consider the following points:

- Create a view using WITH SCHEMABINDING

- The indexed view base objects cannot include other views

- You must reference base objects with two-part names (schema.object_name)

- You must create a clustered index on the indexed view

- The SELECT statement cannot include the UNION keyword or any subqueries

- The LEFT, RIGHT, or FULL OUTER joins are not allowed for indexed view queries

Indexed view example

To create an indexed view, first create a view. Use the following code to do so:

```
USE [AdventureWorks2012];
GO

CREATE VIEW [Sales].[vIndividualEmployeeIndexedViews]
WITH SCHEMABINDING
AS
SELECT  p.[Title] ,
p.[FirstName] + SPACE(1)
+ p.[MiddleName] + SPACE(1)
+ p.[LastName] AS [FullName] ,
e.[JobTitle] ,
d.[Name] AS [Department] ,
d.[GroupName] ,
dhist.[StartDate]
FROM [HumanResources].[Employee] e
INNER JOIN [HumanResources].[EmployeeDepartmentHistory] dhist
ON e.[BusinessEntityID] = dhist.[BusinessEntityID]
AND dhist.[EndDate] IS NULL
INNER JOIN [Person].[Person] p
ON p.[BusinessEntityID] = e.[BusinessEntityID]
INNER JOIN [HumanResources].[Department] d
ON dhist.[DepartmentID] = d.[DepartmentID];
GO
```

Then, using the following code, create a clustered index on the view to make it an indexed view:

```
USE [AdventureWorks2012];
GO

CREATE UNIQUE CLUSTERED INDEX ixc_EmployeeList ON
[Sales].[vIndividualEmployeeIndexedViews]
([FullName], [JobTitle], [StartDate]);
GO
```

Creating and using stored procedures

A stored procedure in SQL Server is a precompiled collection of Transact-SQL statements, variables, and control-of-flow statements typically grouped together to perform a specific task. Stored procedures encapsulate code as a single module for processing. Statements in the procedure usually include DML statements, DDL statements, control-of-flow statements, comments, and calls to .NET Framework CLR methods. The code within a stored procedure is executed as a single unit or batch. The benefit of this is that the network traffic is greatly reduced as several Transact-SQL statements contained in the stored procedure are not required to travel through the network individually. Only the name of the stored procedure and its parameters are transmitted over the network.

The stored procedure runs faster than ad hoc Transact-SQL batches, especially when used in repetitive tasks. This is because SQL Server always caches a stored procedure execution plan in an area of SQL Server memory called procedure cache, and it is likely to remain in the procedure cache (provided there is enough memory available; unless run with RECOMPILE option) and be reused, while ad hoc SQL plans created when running ad hoc Transact-SQL statements might or might not be stored in the procedure cache. Therefore, SQL Server does not retrieve and reload the stored procedure from disk and nor does it parse, optimize, and compile the stored procedure each time it runs.

 You can run DBCC FREEPROCCACHE to manually clear the procedure cache.

Since database operations can be performed within stored procedures, they provide a high level of security. Instead of access granted to the underlying object, permission can be granted for the stored procedure.

The stored procedure allows modular programming, which allows you to break database procedures down into smaller, more manageable pieces.

You can create stored procedures that accept input parameters and return values and status information. Stored procedures use variables for internal temporary data storage, input parameters, and output parameters.

 You can create stored procedures in any SQL Server database except the resource database.

Microsoft SQL Server 2014 has four types of stored procedures, listed as follows:

- **User-defined stored procedures**: These are procedures you write using the CREATE PROCEDURE statement.

- **Natively compiled stored procedures**: These are user-defined stored procedures that operate on memory-optimized tables. Though natively compiled stored procedures are written in Transact-SQL, they are actually compiled to highly efficient machine code. This maximizes the runtime performance of certain workloads and types of queries because the generated machine code only contains exactly what is needed to run the request, and nothing more.

- **System stored procedures**: These are the procedures shipped with SQL Server as part of the default installation. The system stored procedures are used to perform administrative procedures. System stored procedures have names that are prefixed with sp_.

- **Temporary stored procedures**: These are like normal stored procedures, but they do not exist permanently. Instead, temporary stored procedures have a life and limited accessibility, depending on their type. Temporary stored procedures reside inside tempdb. We can create two types of temporary stored procedures: local and global. The name of a local temporary stored procedure must begin with a single number sign (#), and the name of the global temporary stored procedure must begin with two number signs (##).

  Local temporary stored procedures are only available to the user session that created the stored procedure. Therefore, SQL Server removes local temporary stored procedures when the user session ends. On the other hand, global temporary stored procedures are available for all user sessions after their creation. SQL Server removes global temporary stored procedures once all user sessions that refer to it are disconnected.

- **Extended user-defined stored procedures**: These are the routines you write in a programming language, which are compiled as a **dynamic link library (DLL)** file. We write them using the SQL Server Extended Stored Procedure API.

- **CLR stored procedures**: These are the procedures you write using the .NET framework programming language.

> Extended user-defined stored procedures have been replaced by CLR stored procedures. A detailed discussion of CLR stored procedures is beyond the scope of this chapter. For more information about CLR stored procedures, see *CLR Stored Procedure* at http://msdn.microsoft. com/en-us/library/ms131094.aspx.

This chapter only focuses on user-defined stored procedures.

Creating a stored procedure

Now that we understand the purpose of stored procedures, let's take a look at the syntax of the CREATE PROCEDURE statement. Have a look at the following code:

```
CREATE { PROC | PROCEDURE } [schema_name.] procedure_name [ ; number ]
[ { @parameter [ type_schema_name. ] data_type }
[ VARYING ] [ = default ] [ OUT | OUTPUT ] [READONLY]
] [ ,...n ]
[ WITH <procedure_option> [ ,...n ] ]
[ FOR REPLICATION ]
AS { [ BEGIN ] sql_statement [;] [ ...n ] [ END ] } [;]
<procedure_option> ::=
[ ENCRYPTION ]
[ RECOMPILE ]
[ NATIVE_COMPILATION ]
[SCHEMABINDING]
[ EXECUTE AS Clause ]
```

The following are the arguments of the CREATE PROCEDURE statement:

- schema_name: This specifies the name of the schema in which you are creating the stored procedure.

- procedure_name: This specifies the name of the stored procedure; it must be unique within the schema.

- @parameter data_type: This defines the stored procedure parameters.

- procedure_option: These are used to further define the procedure. The following are the available options:

    ◦ ENCRYPTION: This encrypts the text of the CREATE PROCEDURE statement.

    ◦ SCHEMABINDING: This binds the stored procedure to the underlying base objects, meaning users cannot modify the underlying base objects in any way that affects the stored procedure definition. This option is supported only for natively compiled stored procedures.

    ◦ NATIVE_COMPILATION: This makes the stored procedure a natively compiled procedure.

    ◦ EXECUTE AS: This specifies the context under which the stored procedure executes. We can set the execute context as CALLER, SELF, OWNER, or as a username to identify a specific user.

    ◦ WITH RECOMPILE: This recompiles stored procedures each time it runs.

You can also recompile the stored procedure either by executing a stored procedure with the WITH RECOMPILE option or by running a sp_recompile stored procedure.

- NOT FOR REPLICATION: This specifies that the stored procedure cannot be executed on the subscribing server.

- AS: This specifies the SQL statements (for Transact-SQL procedures) or module identifier (for CLR procedures) used to define a stored procedure.

Here is an example of a stored procedure:

```
USE [AdventureWorks2012];
GO

CREATE PROCEDURE [HumanResources].[uspUpdateEmployeeInfo]
    @BusinessEntityID [int],
    @NationalIDNumber [nvarchar](15),
    @BirthDate [datetime],
    @MaritalStatus [nchar](1),
    @Gender [nchar](1)
WITH EXECUTE AS CALLER
AS
BEGIN
    SET NOCOUNT ON;

    BEGIN TRY
        UPDATE [HumanResources].[Employee]
        SET [NationalIDNumber] = @NationalIDNumber
            , [BirthDate] = @BirthDate
            , [MaritalStatus] = @MaritalStatus
            , [Gender] = @Gender
        WHERE [BusinessEntityID] = @BusinessEntityID;
    END TRY
    BEGIN CATCH
        EXECUTE [dbo].[uspLogError];
    END CATCH;
END;
GO
```

 Use SET NOCOUNT ON within stored procedures to increase performance. This is because, when specified, this statement does not return the number of rows affected.

For a natively compiled stored procedure example, first create a memory-optimized table called `Sales.SalesOrderDetail_MO` in the `AdventureWorks2012` database. To create this table, run the following code snippet:

```
USE [master];
GO

ALTER DATABASE [AdventureWorks2012]
ADD FILEGROUP [AW_MEMORYOPTIMIZED]
CONTAINS MEMORY_OPTIMIZED_DATA;

ALTER DATABASE [AdventureWorks2012]
ADD FILE (NAME='AdventureWorks2012_MemoryOptimized',
FILENAME='C:\SQLData\AdventureWorks2012_MO.ndf')
TO FILEGROUP [AW_MemoryOptimized];
GO

USE [AdventureWorks2012];
GO

CREATE TABLE Sales.SalesOrderDetail_MO (
    [SalesOrderID] [int] NOT NULL
  ,[SalesOrderDetailID] [int] NOT NULL
  ,[CarrierTrackingNumber] [nvarchar](25) NULL
  ,[OrderQty] [smallint] NOT NULL
  ,[ProductID] [int] NOT NULL
  ,[SpecialOfferID] [int] NOT NULL
  ,[UnitPrice] [money] NOT NULL
  ,[UnitPriceDiscount] [money] NOT NULL
  ,[LineTotal] [money]
  ,[rowguid] [uniqueidentifier] NOT NULL
  ,[ModifiedDate] [datetime]
  ,CONSTRAINT
  [PK_SalesOrderDetail_SalesOrderID_SalesOrderDetailID2] PRIMARY
  KEY NONCLUSTERED HASH (
    [SalesOrderID]
    ,[SalesOrderDetailID]) WITH (BUCKET_COUNT = 20000))
  WITH (MEMORY_OPTIMIZED = ON
    ,DURABILITY = SCHEMA_AND_DATA);
GO
```

Next, enter and execute the following T-SQL code to copy the data from `Sales.SalesOrderDetail` to our memory-optimized table, `Sales.SalesOrderDetail_MO`:

```
USE [AdventureWorks2012];
GO

INSERT INTO [Sales].[SalesOrderDetail_MO]
SELECT [SalesOrderID]
      ,[SalesOrderDetailID]
```

```
            , [CarrierTrackingNumber]
            , [OrderQty]
            , [ProductID]
            , [SpecialOfferID]
            , [UnitPrice]
            , [UnitPriceDiscount]
            , [LineTotal]
            , [rowguid]
            , [ModifiedDate]
    FROM [Sales] . [SalesOrderDetail];
GO
```

Now that we have created a memory-optimized table in the AdventureWorks2012 database and copied data into it, we are ready for a natively compiled stored procedure example. To create a natively compiled stored procedure, enter and execute the following T-SQL code to retrieve the orders' detail information from the Sales.SalesOrderDetail_MO table:

```
USE [AdventureWorks2012];
GO

CREATE PROCEDURE RetriveOrderDetail
    @SalesOrderID [int]
    WITH NATIVE_COMPILATION
      , SCHEMABINDING
      , EXECUTE AS OWNER
AS
    BEGIN
      ATOMIC
      WITH (TRANSACTION ISOLATION LEVEL = SNAPSHOT
        , LANGUAGE = 'English')
        SELECT  [SalesOrderID] ,
                [SalesOrderDetailID] ,
                [CarrierTrackingNumber] ,
                [OrderQty] ,
                [ProductID] ,
                [SpecialOfferID] ,
                [UnitPrice] ,
                [UnitPriceDiscount] ,
                [LineTotal] ,
                [rowguid] ,
                [ModifiedDate]
        FROM    [Sales] . [SalesOrderDetail_MO]
        WHERE   [SalesOrderID] = @SalesOrderID;
    END;
GO
```

The Transact-SQL code that actually makes the store procedure a natively compiled procedure is as follows:

```
WITH NATIVE_COMPILATION
,SCHEMABINDING
  ,EXECUTE AS OWNER
AS
BEGIN
  ATOMIC
  WITH (TRANSACTION ISOLATION LEVEL = SNAPSHOT
    ,LANGUAGE = 'English')
```

Modifying a stored procedure

We use a ALTER PROCEDURE statement to modify the stored procedure definition. The following is the ALTER PROCEDURE syntax, which is the same as the CREATE PROCEDURE syntax:

```
ALTER { PROC | PROCEDURE } [schema_name.] procedure_name [ ;
number ]
[ { @parameter [ type_schema_name. ] data_type }
[ VARYING ] [ = default ] [ OUT | OUTPUT ] [READONLY]
] [ ,...n ]
[ WITH <procedure_option> [ ,...n ] ]
[ FOR REPLICATION ]
AS { [ BEGIN ] sql_statement [;] [ ...n ] [ END ] }[;]
<procedure_option> ::=
[ ENCRYPTION ]
[ RECOMPILE ]
[ NATIVE_COMPILATION ]
[ SCHEMABINDING ]
[ EXECUTE AS Clause ]
```

The following is an example of the ALTER PROCEDURE statement:

```
USE [AdventureWorks2012];
GO

ALTER PROCEDURE [HumanResources].[uspUpdateEmployeeInfo]
    @BusinessEntityID [int],
    @NationalIDNumber [nvarchar](15),
    @BirthDate [datetime],
    @MaritalStatus [nchar](1),
    @Gender [nchar](1)
WITH EXECUTE AS CALLER
AS
BEGIN
```

```
    SET NOCOUNT ON;

    BEGIN TRY
        UPDATE [HumanResources].[Employee]
        SET [NationalIDNumber] = @NationalIDNumber
            ,[BirthDate] = @BirthDate
            ,[MaritalStatus] = @MaritalStatus
            ,[Gender] = @Gender
        WHERE [BusinessEntityID] = @BusinessEntityID;
    END TRY
    BEGIN CATCH
        EXECUTE [dbo].[uspLogError];
    END CATCH;
END;
GO
```

> Note here that the operation ALTER PROCEDURE is not supported with natively compiled stored procedures.

Dropping a stored procedure

We use the DROP PROCEDURE statement to permanently delete a stored procedure. The DROP PROCEDURE statement syntax is as follows:

```
DROP PROC[EDURE] [schema.]procedure_name
```

The following is an example of the DROP PROCEDURE statement:

```
USE [AdventureWorks2012];
GO

DROP PROCEDURE [HumanResources].[uspUpdateEmployeeInfo];
GO
```

The following are the steps to drop a stored procedure in SSMS 2014:

1. In **Object Explorer**, expand the Databases folder.
2. Expand the database where the stored procedure you want to delete exists.
3. Expand Programmability.
4. Expand Stored Procedures.
5. In Stored Procedures, right-click on the procedure and choose **Delete** from the context menu.
6. SQL Server prompts you to verify your action. Click on **OK** to confirm.

Viewing stored procedures

The following are the steps to view stored procedures in SSMS 2014:

1. In **Object Explorer**, expand the `Databases` folder.

2. Expand the database whose stored procedures you want to view.

3. Expand `Programmability`.

4. Expand `Stored Procedures`. We can now view the stored procedures, as shown in the following screenshot:

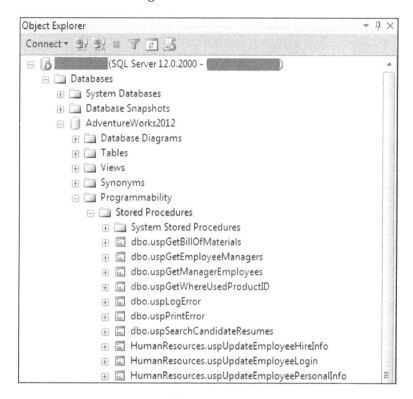

You can also either use the `sp_helptext` system stored procedure or query the `sys.sql_modules` or `sys.syscomments` system view to view the definition of a stored procedure and the statement that was used to create the procedure. (The `sp_helptext` system stored procedure and the `sys.syscomments` system view can also be used to print the definition of a trigger, a view, a rule, or a default.)

You cannot use the sp_helptext system stored procedure and nor can you query the sys.sql_modules and sys.syscomments system views to view the stored procedure definition if a stored procedure was created using the WITH ENCRYPTION option.

Executing stored procedures

Although you can run a stored procedure by simply typing in the name of the stored procedure in SSMS 2014 Query Editor, this is not the recommended way to run the stored procedure. The recommended way is to use the EXECUTE keyword followed by a stored procedure. The syntax for this is as follows:

```
EXECUTE | EXEC procedure_name [parameter1, parameter2, n...]
```

For example, enter and execute the following T-SQL code in SSMS 2014 Query Editor to execute the dbo.uspGetWhereUsedProductID stored procedure:

```
USE [AdventureWorks2012]
GO

DECLARE @RC INT
DECLARE @StartProductID INT = 20
DECLARE @CheckDate DATETIME = CURRENT_TIMESTAMP - 40

EXECUTE @RC = [dbo].[uspGetWhereUsedProductID] @StartProductID,
@CheckDate;
GO
```

Creating and using user-defined functions

User-defined functions (UDFs) are similar to stored procedures, except that they do not support OUTPUT parameters. Instead, a user-defined function returns a value. The type of value returned depends on the type of function. One of the two most notable differences between stored procedures and user-defined functions is that user-defined functions can be used in the SELECT statement, and you can join them to tables, views, CTE and even other functions. The second difference is that you can perform DML operations within stored procedures, but you cannot perform DML operations within user-defined functions.

We primarily use functions to perform logic and complex functions. SQL Server supports Transact-SQL and CLR user-defined functions. The difference between the two is that a Transact-SQL user-defined function is based on Transact-SQL statements and a CLR user-defined function is based on a registered assembly method. In general, CLR user-defined functions are more suitable for computational tasks, string manipulation, and business logic, while Transact-SQL functions are more suitable for data-access-intensive logic.

 A detailed discussion of CLR user-defined function is beyond the scope of this chapter. For help with this, see *Create CLR Functions* at http://msdn.microsoft.com/en-us/library/ms189876.aspx.

The advantages of using functions are the same as those of using stored procedures: modular programming support, reduced network traffic, and faster execution.

Microsoft SQL Server 2014 allows you to create two types of functions: scalar and table-valued. A scalar user-defined function returns a single value, while a table-valued function returns a table that results from a SELECT statement.

Creating user-defined functions

We use the CREATE FUNCTION statement to create a user-defined function. The CREATE FUNCTION syntax varies depending on the type of function you create.

Creating a user-defined scalar function

The syntax to create a user-defined scalar function is as follows:

```
CREATE FUNCTION [ schema_name. ] function_name
( [ { @parameter_name [ AS ][ type_schema_name. ]
parameter_data_type
[ = default ] [ READONLY ] }
[ ,...n ]])
RETURNS return_data_type
[ WITH <function_option> [ ,...n ] ]
[ AS ]
BEGIN
function_body
RETURN scalar_expression
END [ ; ]
```

The following describes the arguments of the CREATE FUNCTION statement:

- schema_name: This specifies the name of the schema in which you are creating the function.

- function_name: This specifies the name of the function; it must be unique within the schema.

- @parameter data_type: This defines the function input parameters.

- WITH <function_option>: These are used to further define the function options. The following are these options:

    ° ENCRYPTION: This encrypts the text of the CREATE FUNCTION statement.

    ° SCHEMABINDING: This binds the function to the underlying base objects, meaning users cannot modify the underlying base object in any way that affects the function definition.

    ° EXECUTE AS: This specifies the context under which the stored procedure executes. We can set the execute context as CALLER, SELF, OWNER, or as a username to identify a specific user.

- RETURNS: This sets the return value data type; we will use scalar data types only for scalar-valued functions.

- sql_statements: These are the statements that generate the return value.

- RETURN: This returns the value result.

For example, run the following Transact-SQL code to create the dbo.fnIsWeekday user-defined scalar function within the AdventureWorks2012 database:

```
USE [AdventureWorks2012];
GO

CREATE FUNCTION dbo.fnIsWeekday ( @p_date [datetime] )
RETURNS [bit]
AS
    BEGIN
        DECLARE @weekday [bit]
        IF ( SELECT DATENAME(dw, @p_date)
            ) IN ( N'Friday', N'Saturday', N'Sunday' )
            BEGIN
                SET @weekday = 0
            END
        ELSE
            BEGIN
                SET @weekday = 1
            END
        RETURN (@weekday)
    END;
GO
```

This user-defined scalar function accepts an input parameter (@p_date) and returns 1 if it is a weekend date and 0 if it is not a weekend date. Moreover, this function definition also includes control-of-flow statements.

 Obviously, you need to provide a date to use this user-defined scalar function.

Using a user-defined scalar function

You can use user-defined scalar function in the same way you use system scalar functions. For example, to use the above user-defined scalar function, run the following code in SSMS 2014 Query Editor:

```
USE [AdventureWorks2012];
GO


SELECT dbo.fnIsWeekday ('June 23, 2014');
GO
```

The preceding code snippet returns 1 as June 23, 2014, a weekday. The following screenshot shows the result of the preceding code:

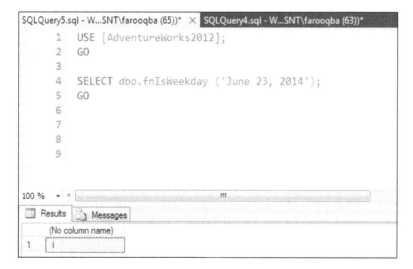

Creating a user-defined table-valued function

We can create two types of table-valued functions: inline table-valued functions and multistatement table-valued functions. The inline table-valued function simply returns a result set from a query, and the multistatement table-valued function offers the ability to include logic within the body of the function and returns the result set on the basis of that logic. The syntax to create both types of table-valued functions are as follows:

- The syntax for an inline table-valued function is as follows:

```
CREATE FUNCTION [ schema_name. ] function_name
( [ { @parameter_name [ AS ] [ type_schema_name. ]
parameter_data_type
[ = default ] [ READONLY ] }
[ ,...n ]])
RETURNS TABLE
[ WITH <function_option> [ ,...n ] ]
[ AS ]
RETURN [ ( ] select_stmt [ ) ][ ; ]
```

- The syntax for a multistatement table-valued function is as follows:

```
CREATE FUNCTION [ schema_name. ] function_name
( [ { @parameter_name [ AS ] [ type_schema_name. ]
parameter_data_type
[ = default ] [READONLY] }
[ ,...n ]])
RETURNS @return_variable TABLE <table_type_definition>
[ WITH <function_option> [ ,...n ] ]
[ AS ]
BEGIN
function_body
RETURN
END[ ; ]
```

The parameters of the CREATE FUNCTION statement for both types of user-defined table-valued functions are the same as the CREATE FUNCTION statement of user-defined scalar functions, except that the user-defined table-valued functions return a result set rather than a single value.

Inline table-valued function example

Here is an example of an inline table-valued function:

```
USE [AdventureWorks2012];
GO


CREATE FUNCTION [dbo].[GetEmployeeDetails] (@p_employeeid [int])
RETURNS TABLE
AS
RETURN
(
WITH [CTE_EmployeeInfo]
AS
(
SELECT e.[BusinessEntityID], p.[Title], p.[FirstName] ,
p.[MiddleName] , p.[LastName] , p.[Suffix] , e.[JobTitle] ,
pp.[PhoneNumber] , pnt.[Name] AS [PhoneNumberType] ,
ea.[EmailAddress] , p.[EmailPromotion] , a.[AddressLine1] ,
a.[AddressLine2] ,
a.[City], sp.[Name] AS [StateProvinceName] , a.[PostalCode] ,
cr.[Name] AS [CountryRegionName]
FROM [HumanResources].[Employee] e
INNER JOIN [Person].[Person] p ON p.[BusinessEntityID] =
e.[BusinessEntityID]
INNER JOIN [Person].[BusinessEntityAddress] bea ON
bea.[BusinessEntityID] = e.[BusinessEntityID]
INNER JOIN [Person].[Address] a ON a.[AddressID] = bea.[AddressID]
INNER JOIN [Person].[StateProvince] sp ON sp.[StateProvinceID] =
a.[StateProvinceID]
INNER JOIN [Person].[CountryRegion] cr ON cr.[CountryRegionCode] =
sp.[CountryRegionCode]
LEFT OUTER JOIN [Person].[PersonPhone] pp ON pp.BusinessEntityID =
p.[BusinessEntityID]
LEFT OUTER JOIN [Person].[PhoneNumberType] pnt ON
pp.[PhoneNumberTypeID] = pnt.[PhoneNumberTypeID]
LEFT OUTER JOIN [Person].[EmailAddress] ea ON p.[BusinessEntityID]
= ea.[BusinessEntityID]
)
SELECT * FROM [CTE_EmployeeInfo]
WHERE [BusinessEntityID] = @p_employeeid
)
GO
```

This user-defined scalar function accepts an input parameter (@p_employeeid) and returns the employee details of the specified employee.

Multistatement table-valued function example

Here is an example of a multistatement table-valued function:

```
USE [AdventureWorks2012];
GO

CREATE FUNCTION [dbo].[ufnRetrieveContactInformation]
(@p_contactid [int])
RETURNS @ContactDetails TABLE
( -- Columns returned by the function
[ContactID] [int] PRIMARY KEY NOT NULL ,
[Title] [nvarchar](8) NULL ,
[FirstName] [nvarchar](50) NULL ,
[MiddleName] [nvarchar](50) NULL ,
[LastName] [nvarchar](50) NULL ,
[JobTitle] [nvarchar](50) NULL ,
[ContactType] [nvarchar](50) NULL )
AS
BEGIN
IF @p_contactid IS NOT NULL
BEGIN
INSERT  INTO @ContactDetails ([ContactID], [Title],  [FirstName],
[MiddleName],  [LastName], [ContactType])
SELECT  [BusinessEntityID], [Title], [FirstName], [MiddleName],
[LastName], CASE [PersonType] WHEN N'EM' THEN N'Employee' WHEN
N'SP' THEN N'Employee' WHEN N'VC' THEN N'Vendor Contact' WHEN
N'SC' THEN N'Store Contact' WHEN N'IN' THEN N'Consumer' ELSE
N'General Contact' END
FROM    [Person].[Person]
WHERE   [BusinessEntityID] = @p_contactid;

IF EXISTS (SELECT  * FROM [Person].[Person] p WHERE
p.[BusinessEntityID] = @p_contactid AND p.[PersonType] IN ( N'EM',
N'SP' ))
BEGIN
UPDATE  @ContactDetails
SET [JobTitle] = (SELECT e.[JobTitle] FROM [Person].[Person] p
INNER JOIN [HumanResources].[Employee] e ON e.[BusinessEntityID] =
p.[BusinessEntityID] AND p.[BusinessEntityID] = @p_contactid);
```

```
END;

IF EXISTS (SELECT  * FROM [Person].[Person] p WHERE
p.[BusinessEntityID] = @p_contactid AND p.[PersonType] = N'VC')
BEGIN
UPDATE  @ContactDetails
SET [JobTitle] = (SELECT ct.[Name] FROM [Person].[Person] p INNER
JOIN [Person].[BusinessEntityContact] bec ON bec.[PersonID] =
p.[BusinessEntityID] AND p.[BusinessEntityID] = @p_contactid INNER
JOIN [Person].[ContactType] ct ON ct.[ContactTypeID] =
bec.[ContactTypeID]);
END;

IF EXISTS (SELECT  * FROM [Person].[Person] p WHERE
p.[BusinessEntityID] = @p_contactid AND p.[PersonType] = N'SC')
BEGIN
UPDATE  @ContactDetails
SET [JobTitle] = (SELECT ct.[Name] FROM [Person].[Person] p INNER
JOIN [Person].[BusinessEntityContact] bec ON bec.[PersonID] =
p.[BusinessEntityID] AND p.[BusinessEntityID] = @p_contactid INNER
JOIN [Person].[ContactType] ct ON ct.[ContactTypeID] =
bec.[ContactTypeID] INNER JOIN [Sales].[Store]  s ON
bec.[BusinessEntityID] = s.[BusinessEntityID]);
END;

IF EXISTS (SELECT  * FROM [Person].[Person] p WHERE
p.[BusinessEntityID] = @p_contactid AND p.[PersonType] = N'IN')
BEGIN
UPDATE  @ContactDetails
SET [JobTitle] = (SELECT   NULL FROM [Person].[Person] p INNER
JOIN [Sales].[Customer] c ON c.[PersonID] = p.[BusinessEntityID]
AND p.[BusinessEntityID] = @p_contactid AND c.[StoreID] IS NULL );
END;
END;
RETURN;
END;
GO
```

This user-defined scalar function accepts an input parameter (@p_contactid) and returns the title, first name, middle name, last name, job title, and contact type of the specified contact.

Modifying user-defined functions

We use the ALTER FUNCTION statement to modify a function. It uses the same syntax as the CREATE FUNCTION statement.

For scalar-value functions, the syntax is as follows:

```
ALTER FUNCTION [ schema_name. ] function_name
( [ { @parameter_name [ AS ] [ type_schema_name. ]
parameter_data_type
[ = default ] [ READONLY ] }
[ ,...n ]])
RETURNS return_data_type
[ WITH <function_option> [ ,...n ] ]
[ AS ]
BEGIN
function_body
RETURN scalar_expression
END [ ; ]
```

For inline table-valued function, the syntax is as follows:

```
ALTER FUNCTION [ schema_name. ] function_name
( [ { @parameter_name [ AS ] [ type_schema_name. ]
parameter_data_type
[ = default ] [ READONLY ] }
[ ,...n ]])
RETURNS TABLE
[ WITH <function_option> [ ,...n ] ]
[ AS ]
RETURN [ ( ] select_stmt [ ) ] [ ; ]
```

For multistatement table-valued functions, the syntax is as follows:

```
ALTER FUNCTION [ schema_name. ] function_name
( [ { @parameter_name [ AS ] [ type_schema_name. ]
parameter_data_type
[ = default ] [READONLY] }
[ ,...n ]])
RETURNS @return_variable TABLE <table_type_definition>
[ WITH <function_option> [ ,...n ] ]
[ AS ]
BEGIN
function_body
RETURN
END [ ; ]
```

Using a user-defined table-valued function

You can use a user-defined table-valued function in the same way you use tables or views. For example, to use the preceding user-defined table-valued functions, run the following code in SSMS 2014 Query Editor:

```
USE [AdventureWorks2012]
GO

SELECT *
FROM [dbo].[GetEmployeeDetails](92);
GO

SELECT *
FROM [dbo].[ufnRetrieveContactInformation] (89);
GO
```

Dropping user-defined functions

We use the DROP FUNCTION statement to permanently delete a user-defined function. The DROP FUNCTION statement syntax is as follows:

```
DROP PROC[EDURE] [schema.]function_name
```

The following is an example of the DROP FUNCTION statement:

```
USE [AdventureWorks2012];
GO

DROP FUNCTION [dbo].[ufnRetrieveContactInformation];
GO
```

The following are the steps to drop a function in SSMS 2014:

1. In **Object Explorer**, expand the Databases folder.
2. Expand the database where the function you want to delete exists.
3. Expand Programmability.
4. Expand Functions.
5. Expand the appropriate user-defined function folder.
6. Right-click on the function you want to delete, and then choose **Delete** from the context menu.
7. SQL Server prompts you to verify your action. Click on **OK** to confirm.

Viewing user-defined functions

To view functions in SSMS 2014, perform the following steps:

1. In **Object Explorer**, expand the `Databases` folder.

2. Expand the database for which you want to view functions.

3. Expand `Programmability`.

4. Expand `Functions`. The following screenshot shows the functions in SSMS 2014:

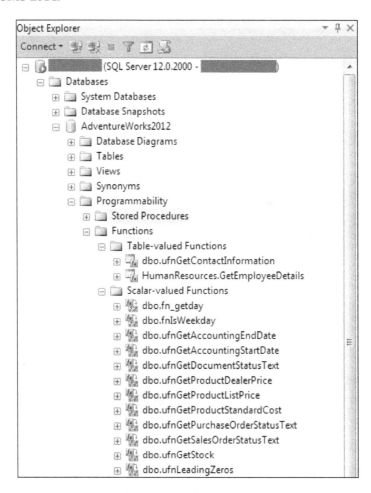

You can also either use the `sp_helptext` system stored procedure or query the `sys.sql_modules` or `sys.syscomments` system view to view the definition of a function and the statement that was used to create a function.

 If a function was created using `WITH ENCRYPTION`, you cannot use the `sp_helptext` system stored procedure and nor can you query the `sys.sql_modules` and `sys.syscomments` system views to view its definition.

Creating and using triggers

A trigger is a special type of stored procedure that fires (executes) in response to an event. We typically use triggers to maintain data integrity rules that are too complicated to implement through constraints and referential integrity. We also use triggers to:

- Implement referential actions, such as cascading deletes
- Maintain an audit trail of changes
- Perform administrative tasks such as auditing and regulating database operations
- Compare data before and after modification
- Implement custom error messages

Triggers cannot support parameters and should not return values or result sets.

Microsoft SQL Server 2014 has two basic trigger types: DML triggers and DDL triggers.

 You can write DDL and DML triggers as Transact-SQL or CLR triggers. In this topic, we will use Transact-SQL to write DDL and DML triggers. For more information about CLR triggers, see *CLR triggers* at `http://msdn.microsoft.com/en-us/library/ms131093.aspx`.

Nested triggers

SQL Server 2014 allows the nesting of DDL and DML triggers if the nested triggers server configuration option is enabled. The `nested triggers` option allows triggers to call themselves recursively. For example, one trigger changes a table to activate another trigger, which activates another trigger, and so on. SQL Server has a maximum nesting depth of 32.

By default, the `nested triggers` option is disabled. To enable this, use the `sp_configure` system stored procedure as follows:

```
USE [master];
GO

EXEC sp_configure 'show advanced options', 1;
GO
-- To update the currently configured value for advanced options.
RECONFIGURE;
GO


-- To enable the nested trigger feature.
EXEC sp_configure 'nested triggers', 1;
GO


-- To update the currently configured value for this feature.
RECONFIGURE;
GO
```

Nested triggers require careful planning because they can result in multiple changes in the same column or even changes in multiple tables. Nested triggers can produce unexpected results.

Instead of nesting triggers, you may find it more appropriate to have one trigger perform all of the required actions. This is usually easier to manage and results in an easier-to-maintain solution.

Recursive triggers

A trigger that can activate itself is called a recursive trigger. There are two types of recursion: direct and indirect recursion. Direct recursion occurs when a trigger directly activates itself, while indirect recursion occurs when the trigger activates another trigger, which then activates the first trigger. SQL Server 2014 disables recursive triggers by default.

DML triggers

DML triggers fire in response to any combination of INSERT, UPDATE, or DELETE events on a specific table. We cannot create DML triggers on system tables. Moreover, you cannot use the following statements in DML triggers: CREATE DATABASE, ALTER DATABASE, DROP DATABASES, RESTORE DATABASE, RESTORE LOG, RECONFIGURE, DISK INIT, DISK RESIZE, and SHUTDOWN.

There are two types of DML triggers, listed as follows, based on when the code in the trigger executes:

- AFTER: This fires after processing the data manipulation statement. SQL Server does not allow you to create AFTER triggers on views.

- INSTEAD OF: This fires before the data manipulation statement executes, and the code in the trigger runs instead of the statement.

Inserted and deleted logical tables

The inserted and deleted tables are special tables accessible from within the bodies of DML triggers only. The tables reside in memory and contain the rows affected by the DML statement that caused the trigger to fire.

Creating DML triggers

We use the CREATE TRIGGER statement to create triggers. The syntax of the CREATE TRIGGER statement is as follows:

```
CREATE TRIGGER [ schema_name . ]trigger_name
ON { table | view }
[ WITH <dml_trigger_option> [ ,...n ] ]
{ FOR | AFTER | INSTEAD OF }
{ [ INSERT ] [ , ] [ UPDATE ] [ , ] [ DELETE ] }
[ NOT FOR REPLICATION ]
AS { sql_statement [ ; ] [ ,...n ] | EXTERNAL NAME <method
specifier [ ; ] > }
<dml_trigger_option> ::=
[ ENCRYPTION ]
[ EXECUTE AS Clause ]
<method_specifier> ::=
assembly_name.class_name.method_name
```

The following describes the arguments of the CREATE FUNCTION statement:

- schema_name: This specifies the name of the schema in which you are creating the trigger.

- trigger_name: This specifies the name of the trigger; it must be unique within the schema.

- ON {table | view}: This specifies the name of the table or view on which you are creating the trigger.

- `trigger_options`: These are used to further define the trigger. The options are as follows:
  - ° ENCRYPTION: This encrypts the text of the CREATE TRIGGER statement.
  - ° EXECUTE AS: This specifies the context under which the trigger executes. We can set the execute context as CALLER, SELF, OWNER, or as a username to identify a specific user.
- FOR | AFTER | INSTEAD OF: This specifies the DML trigger type.
- NOT FOR REPLICATION: This specifies that the specified trigger is not executed when the table is updated or modified through replication.
- `sql_statements`: This specifies the statements that will generate the result table by trigger.

Here is a basic example of the DML trigger:

```
USE [AdventureWorks2012];
GO

CREATE TRIGGER [Production].[WorkOrder_after_trigger] ON
[Production].[WorkOrder]
AFTER INSERT
AS
BEGIN
DECLARE @Count INT;

SET @Count = @@ROWCOUNT;
IF @Count = 0
RETURN;

SET NOCOUNT ON;
INSERT INTO [Production].[TransactionHistory]
( [ProductID] ,
    [ReferenceOrderID] ,
    [TransactionType] ,
    [TransactionDate] ,
    [Quantity] ,
    [ActualCost]
)
SELECT  inserted.[ProductID] ,
        inserted.[WorkOrderID] ,
        'W' ,
        GETDATE() ,
        inserted.[OrderQty] ,
        0
FROM    inserted;
END;
GO
```

Modifying a DML trigger

We use the ALTER TRIGGER statement to modify a function. It uses the same syntax as the CREATE TRIGGER statement. The ALTER TRIGGER statement syntax is as follows:

```
ALTER TRIGGER [ schema_name . ]trigger_name
ON { table | view }
[ WITH <dml_trigger_option> [ ,...n ] ]
{ FOR | AFTER | INSTEAD OF }
{ [ INSERT ] [ , ] [ UPDATE ] [ , ] [ DELETE ] }
[ NOT FOR REPLICATION ]
AS { sql_statement [ ; ] [ ,...n ] | EXTERNAL NAME <method
specifier [ ; ] > }
<dml_trigger_option> ::=
[ ENCRYPTION ]
[ EXECUTE AS Clause ]
<method_specifier> ::=
assembly_name.class_name.method_name
```

Dropping a DML trigger

We use the DROP TRIGGER statement to permanently delete a trigger. The DROP TRIGGER statement syntax is as follows:

```
DROP TRIGGER schema.trigger_name
```

Data Definition Language (DDL) triggers

DDL triggers fire in response to data-definition-level events such as creating or dropping objects. DDL triggers can have database- or server-wide scope.

The EVENTDATA function

The EVENTDATA function provides detailed information about the DDL event that caused the DDL trigger to fire. The EVENTDATA function returns a value of type XML.

Creating a DDL trigger

To create a DDL trigger, we execute the CREATE TRIGGER statement using the following syntax:

```
CREATE TRIGGER trigger_name
ON {ALL SERVER | DATABASE }
```

```
WITH <ddl_trigger_option> [,...n]
{FOR | AFTER} {event_type | event_group} [,...n]
AS {sql_statements | EXTERNAL NAME <method_specifier>
```

As you can see, its syntax is the same as the DML trigger CREATE TRIGGER statement. Specify ON ALL SERVER to set the scope of the DDL trigger to the current server and specify ON DATABASE to set the scope of the DDL trigger to the current database. When you create a DDL trigger, you specify either an event or an event group.

For the list of events / event groups that you can use with DDL trigger, refer to *DDL Event Groups* at http://msdn.microsoft.com/en-us/library/bb510452.aspx.

The following is a basic example of the DDL trigger that fires in response to database-level events:

```
CREATE TRIGGER trig_preventDDLOOH ON DATABASE
    FOR DDL_DATABASE_LEVEL_EVENTS
AS
BEGIN
    IF (DATEPART(HOUR, CURRENT_TIMESTAMP) < 8
            OR DATEPART(HOUR, CURRENT_TIMESTAMP) > 17)
PRINT N'You cannot perform DDL outside of normal business hours';
    ROLLBACK;
END
GO
```

This trigger fires and prevents any database-level changes outside normal business hours, that is, 08:00 to 17:00.

Modifying a DDL trigger

To modify a DDL trigger, we execute the ALTER TRIGGER statement using the following syntax:

```
ALTER TRIGGER trigger_name
ON {ALL SERVER | DATABASE }
WITH <ddl_trigger_option> [,...n]
{FOR | AFTER} {event_type | event_group} [,...n]
AS {sql_statements | EXTERNAL NAME <method_specifier>
```

Dropping a DDL trigger

To delete a DDL trigger, we execute the DROP TRIGGER statement using the following syntax:

```
DROP TRIGGER schema.trigger_name
ON {ALL SERVER | DATABASE}
```

Disabling and enabling triggers

We can also enable and disable triggers. To enable a trigger, we use the ENABLE TRIGGER statement as follows:

```
ENABLE TRIGGER [schema.]trigger_name | ALL
ON table_or_view | DATABASE | ALL SERVER
```

To disable a trigger, we use the DISABLE TRIGGER statement as follows:

```
DISABLE TRIGGER [schema.]trigger_name | ALL
ON table_or_view | DATABASE | ALL SERVER
```

We can also use SSMS 2014 to disable or enable a trigger. To enable or disable the trigger, right-click on the trigger and select **Disable** or **Enable**.

Viewing triggers

You can view the DML triggers for an individual table in SSMS 2014 under the table's Triggers folder. We can view DDL triggers by scope. For database triggers, expand the Databases folder, then Programmability and then Database Trigger. For DDL server triggers, expand the server instance, then the Server Objects folder, and then Triggers.

You can either use the sp_helptext system stored procedure or query the following system views to view the definition of DDL and DML triggers:

- sys.triggers: This returns information about all triggers
- sys.servertriggers: This returns information about server-level triggers
- sys.sql_modules: This returns creation information about all triggers

Handling Transact-SQL errors

Like other programming languages, T-SQL provides a sophisticated mechanism that captures and handles errors during execution. The mechanism for handling errors during execution includes the object-oriented-programming-style TRY...CATCH construct. When writing Transact-SQL batches and programmable objects, we wrap the Transact-SQL statements to be executed within a TRY block, and at runtime, if an error occurs, control is sent to the CATCH block. We enclose error-handling code within the CATCH block. The syntax for the TRY...CATCH construct is as follows:

```
BEGIN TRY
{ sql_statement  |statement_block}
END TRY
BEGIN CATCH
[{ sql_statement  |statement_block}]
END CATCH
```

Only errors with severity between 11 and 19 cause the CATCH block to execute. SQL Server treats errors with lower severity as informational messages. Errors with severity 20 or higher usually terminate the connection. If they do terminate the connection, SQL Server does not execute the Transact-SQL code within the CATCH block. If they do not terminate the connection, SQL Server executes the Transact-SQL code within the CATCH block.

You can use the following scalar functions within the CATCH block to retrieve the information about the error that caused the CATCH block to execute:

- ERROR_NUMBER(): This returns the error number

> The @@ERROR function also returns the error number if the previous Transact-SQL statement encountered an error during execution. It returns 0 if the previous Transact-SQL statement is executed without any error.

- ERROR_MESSAGE(): This returns the textual description of the error
- ERROR_SEVERITY(): This returns the error severity
- ERROR_STATE(): This returns the error state number

> You can use the state number in conjunction with the error number when looking for information about the error in the Knowledge Base.

- `ERROR_LINE()`: This returns the line number of the Transact-SQL statement on which the error occurred
- `ERROR_PROCEDURE()`: This returns the name of the stored procedure or trigger where the error occurred

You can use THROW with the TRY block to raise an exception and transfer execution to the CATCH block. The THROW statement must end with a semicolon (;). The syntax for the THROW statement is as follows:

```
THROW [{ error_number | @local_variable },
{ message | @local_variable },

{ state | @local_variable }] [ ; ]
```

We use the RAISERROR statement to instruct SQL Server to send an error to a client application. We typically use the RAISERROR statement for user-defined errors. The syntax for the RAISERROR statement is as follows:

```
RAISERROR ( { msg_id | msg_str | @local_variable }
    { ,severity ,state }
    [ ,argument [ ,...n ] ] )
    [ WITH option [ ,...n ] ]
```

The following sections discuss a few examples of the TRY...CATCH construct.

An example of TRY...CATCH

The following code snippet illustrates a simple TRY...CATCH block:

```
BEGIN TRY
    SELECT  50 / 0
END TRY
BEGIN CATCH
    SELECT  @@ERROR AS [@@ERROR]
    SELECT  ERROR_NUMBER() AS [ERROR_NUMBER] ,
            ERROR_MESSAGE() AS [ERROR_MESSAGE]
END CATCH
```

Executing this will return the output shown in the following screenshot:

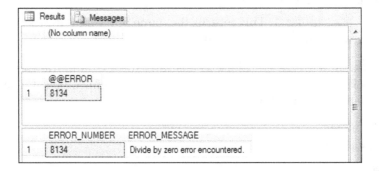

An example of TRY...CATCH with THROW

The following code snippet illustrates a TRY...CATCH expression with a THROW block:

```
BEGIN TRY
    SELECT  50 / 0
END TRY
BEGIN CATCH
    THROW;
END CATCH
```

Executing this will return the output shown in the following screenshot:

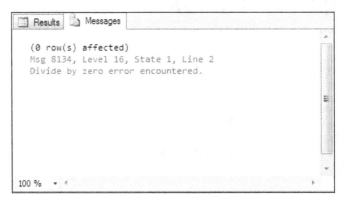

An example of TRY...CATCH with RAISERROR

The following code snippet illustrates a TRY...CATCH expression with a RAISERROR block:

```
BEGIN TRY
    SELECT  50 / 0
END TRY
BEGIN CATCH
    RAISERROR (N'Oops, a divide-by-zero error occurred.', 16, 1)
WITH NOWAIT
END CATCH
```

Executing this will return the output shown in the following screenshot:

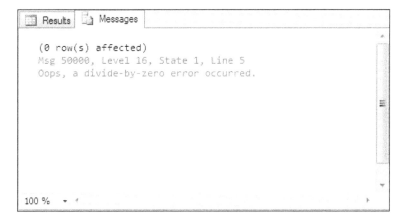

Summary

In this chapter, you declared and used local variables. You learned about control-of-flow statements and learned how to use them to control program execution. You understood the purpose of views, stored procedures, user-defined functions, and triggers, as well as understood the guidelines and restrictions to designing each of these programmable objects. You also learned how to design, create, and use views, stored procedures, user-defined functions, and triggers. In the last section, you learned how to handle errors that occur within Transact-SQL batches and programmable objects using the TRY...CATCH construct.

6

Performance Basics

There are many factors that could affect the performance of a SQL Server database, such as the server hardware, the operating system setup, and the configuration of the database. Therefore, optimizing the database performance is often considered to be one of the most difficult tasks that few understand. However, in most situations, you can achieve optimum performance with a relatively small investment of your time and by understanding how SQL Server works.

After completing this chapter, you will be able to do the following:

- Understand the workings of the SQL Server Relational Engine
- Understand the workings of the SQL Server 2014 in-memory engine (Hekaton)
- Understand the use of indexes and how they optimize database performance
- Understand the purpose of SQL Server query optimization statistics
- Understand the use of transactions and locks
- Identify the tools that you can use to troubleshoot the performance of SQL Server Database Engine

Components of SQL Server Database Engine

SQL Server Database Engine has two major components: Relational Engine and Storage Engine. We have already covered the SQL Server Storage Engine architecture in the first chapter of this book. In this section, we'll be covering the SQL Server Relational Engine architecture and other topics to optimize the SQL Server Relational Engine.

The SQL Server Relational Engine architecture

The SQL Server Relational Engine is also known as the query processor because it produces the optimal execution plan for your query or each query stored in a batch or stored procedure. Then, it executes this query plan to deliver the desired results to the client in a format specified in the submitted Transact-SQL statement.

The following diagram outlines the query optimization process:

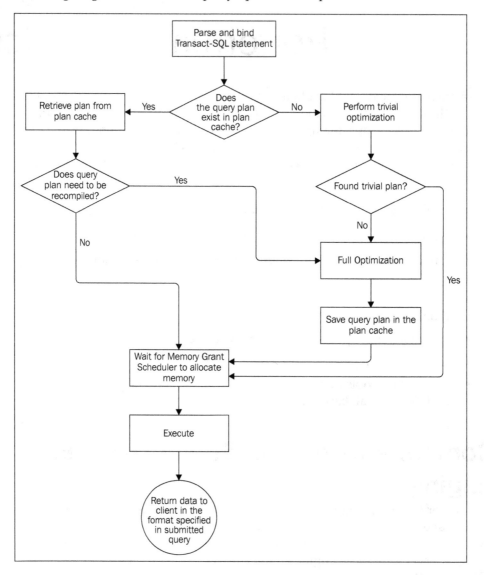

The key phases of the query optimization process are explored in the next sections.

Parsing and binding

The SQL Server Relational Engine includes a command parser that checks the query to make sure that its syntax is valid. If the query has a syntax error, the error is returned to the client through a protocol layer. If the query syntax is valid, the command parser generates a parse tree and proceeds to the algebrizer. The algebrizer's primary function is to perform binding, that is, to validate whether the tables and columns used in the query exist; load the metadata information for the tables and columns; identify all of the data types used for the query; add information about the required implicit data conversions (typecasting) to the algebrizer tree; replace views with definitions; verify whether the GROUP BY and aggregate functions are used in the right place; and perform simple, syntax-based optimizations. The output of this phase is the tree of logical operators that are necessary to carry out the work that the query has requested.

Query optimization

Query optimization is one of the most complex phases of query processing. The first step of this phase is to perform trivial optimization, where SQL Server tries to determine whether a trivial plan for the query exists. A trivial plan is one that has a known, constant CPU and I/O cost. The trivial plan will only exist when the SQL Server optimizer determines that there is only one viable plan to run the query. The SQL Server query optimizer performs trivial optimization based on the complexity of a submitted query. For example, the SQL Server query optimizer creates a trivial query plan for one of the following instances:

- For a SELECT query on a single table with no indexes
- For a SELECT query on a single table with no ORDER BY or GROUP BY clause
- For a SELECT query on a single table with **Search Arguments (SARG)** on a unique key
- For a SELECT query that involves no parameters
- For a SELECT query that uses predefined system functions
- For an INSERT statement using a VALUES clause to insert data into a single table

This is because there is only one viable way to execute such Transact-SQL statements.

So, when you submit a query, the SQL Server query optimizer first determines whether the query plan is trivial. To do this, it investigates the query and relevant metadata to determine whether there is only one viable method to run the query. Due to trivial optimization, the SQL Server query optimizer is able to avoid a lot of the work that is required to initiate and carry out cost-based optimization. If a query has a trivial plan, the SQL Server query optimizer returns the trivial query plan to the query executor and no additional work is required.

If a trivial plan is not available, the SQL Server query optimizer retrieves all of the available statistics for columns and indexes that will help it find the optimal execution plan from the plan cache. At this stage, the SQL Server query optimizer performs more syntactical transformations of the query itself, such as cumulative properties and operations that can be rearranged. After this, the SQL Server query optimizer begins the optimization process.

> A plan cache is an area of memory that is used to store query execution plans. You can use the sys.dm_exec_cached_plans dynamic management view to find query plans that are cached in the SQL Server plan cache. For more information on the columns of this dynamic management view, refer to the *sys.dm_exec_cached_plans (Transact-SQL)* article at http://msdn.microsoft.com/en-us/library/ms187404.aspx.

Initially, the SQL Server query optimizer looks in the plan cache for the simple query plan. The simple query plan is one that usually uses a nested loops join and one index per table. If the SQL Server query optimizer does not find a simple query plan in the plan cache, it then looks for more complex query plan possibilities by analyzing multiple indexes on the table to find a good enough query plan. In a situation where a table is being used in a join and it does not have a suitable index for the query join criteria, the SQL Server query optimizer attempts to seek possibilities for a complex query plan by assessing the cost of using a hash join.

If the SQL Server query optimizer is unable to find the appropriate query plan in the plan cache, it enters into a full cost-based optimization phase. In this phase, the SQL Server query optimizer uses the logical tree to devise every possible way to run the query. If your machine has multiple processors and the cost threshold for parallelism and max degree of parallelism configuration options are configured correctly, the SQL Server query optimizer then creates only the parallel query execution plan for parallel processing.

> The SQL Server query optimizer chooses a nonparallel query plan over a parallel query plan, only when the cost of the least expensive parallel query plan is greater than the cost of the least expensive nonparallel query plan.

The SQL Server query optimizer then chooses the least expensive query plan in terms of the required CPU processing and I/Os, then it passes it along to the query executor for processing.

The reason I used the word "least expensive" here is because the SQL Server query optimizer is a cost-based optimizer. This means that a faster or better query plan might exist in the plan cache, but the query optimizer will always choose the execution plan that it deems will have the lowest cost in terms of the required CPU processing and I/Os.

So, all in all, the main objective of the SQL Server query optimizer is to create a low-cost execution plan, which it then passes along to the query executor for processing.

 You can query the `sys.dm_exec_query_optimizer_info` dynamic management view to see detailed statistics about the operation of the SQL Server query optimizer. For further information on this dynamic management view, refer to the *sys.dm_exec_query_optimizer_info (Transact-SQL)* article at `http://msdn.microsoft.com/en-us/library/ms175002.aspx`.

Query execution and plan caching

After the execution plan is created or retrieved from the plan cache, the SQL Server query executor uses the selected query execution plan and works in conjunction with the storage engine to run the query and return the results to the client through a protocol layer in the format specified in the submitted Transact-SQL statement.

Note that the SQL Server query optimizer may change the estimated execution plan during the actual execution process if the following conditions are met:

- The table and column statistics are out of date
- The nonparallel plan exceeds the threshold for a parallel plan execution
- The data in the underlying query tables changes significantly

In addition, if the underlying table's data, indexes, or statistics change significantly between each run, it results in the recompilation of an execution plan. If not, this estimated plan is then stored in the plan cache.

 At most, SQL Server caches two instances of the query plan in the plan cache at a given time: the parallel execution plan and nonparallel execution plan.

Query plan aging

SQL Server saves each query plan with its age and the cost factor. The cost factor reflects the total cost when compiling the query. The cost factor is incremented by 1 each time that the query plan is referenced. SQL Server does not decrement this cost factor until the size of the plan cache reaches 50 percent of the size of the SQL Server buffer pool. When this happens, and the next time plan cache is accessed, SQL Server decrements the cost factor for all cached query plans by 1. It then periodically cleans the plan cache. This happens in the following situations:

- When the SQL Server buffer pool requires more memory for another object
- When the cost factor of the query plan reaches 0
- When the query plan is not referenced by any connection

The improved design in SQL Server 2014 for the cardinality estimation

Cardinality refers to the number of unique values that exist in the data. To improve the quality of the query plan, Microsoft redesigned the query optimizer cardinality estimator algorithm logic in SQL Server 2014. By default, all databases created with SQL Server 2014 have this feature enabled. For the new cardinality estimator to be enabled on databases that were created with prior versions, the compatibility level of the databases must be set to 120. For more information on the new cardinality estimator, see the *Cardinality Estimation (SQL Server)* article at `http://msdn.microsoft.com/en-us/library/dn600374.aspx`.

Optimizing SQL Server for ad hoc workloads

By default, SQL Server caches all query plans in the plan cache. If your SQL Server is experiencing memory pressure, it is recommended that you optimize SQL Server for ad hoc workloads. You can do this by running the following Transact-SQL code:

```
USE [master];
GO

EXEC [sp_configure] 'show advanced options', 1;
GO

RECONFIGURE;
GO

EXEC [sp_configure] 'optimize for ad hoc workloads', 1;
GO

RECONFIGURE;
```

```
GO

EXEC [sp_configure] 'show advanced options', 0;
GO

RECONFIGURE;
GO
```

Setting this option will not affect plans that are already in the plan cache. This option is only available on SQL Server 2008 and higher SQL Server versions.

Manually clearing the plan cache

If you want to clear the plan cache manually, you need to run DBCC FREEPROCCACHE. You should avoid running this command in a production environment because clearing the plan cache forces queries and stored procedures to be recompiled, which reduces the query performance temporarily.

The SQL Server 2014 in-memory OLTP engine

The SQL Server 2014 in-memory **online transaction processing (OLTP)** engine, previously code-named Hekaton, allows you to create in-memory, optimized OLTP tables within a conventional relational database. It is one of the key, new, performance-related architectural enhancements to SQL Server Database Engine. Like traditional transactions on disk-based tables, the transactions on in-memory-optimized OLTP tables are fully atomic, consistent, isolated, and durable. The in-memory OLTP engine solves problems in high-concurrency situations as it uses data structures that are entirely latch-free (lock-free), which means there are no latches or spinlocks on performance-critical paths in the system. Instead, it uses an optimistic **Multiversion Concurrency Control (MVCC)** technique that provides transaction isolation semantics, which help avoid interference among transactions. Thus, any user process can access any row in a table without acquiring latches or locks.

The combination of these MVCC and latch-free data structures results in a system in which user processes can run without stalling or waiting. In addition, stored procedures that operate on memory-optimized tables, though written in Transact-SQL, are compiled to highly efficient machine code. This maximizes the runtime performance for certain workloads and types of queries because the generated machine code only contains exactly what is needed to run the query, and nothing more. According to Microsoft, some applications can achieve a 50x performance increase only using the in-memory OTLP engine.

There are two main types of in-memory optimized OLTP tables: SCHEMA_AND_DATA and SCHEMA_ONLY. The following is a brief explanation of these:

- SCHEMA_AND_DATA in-memory optimized OLTP tables reside in memory where both the schema of the table and the data persist after SQL Server crashes or restarts

- SCHEMA_ONLY in-memory optimized OLTP tables reside in memory where only the schema of the table persists after SQL Server crashes or restarts

SCHEMA_ONLY in-memory optimized OLTP tables are useful as staging tables for your database application. On the other hand, SCHEMA_AND_DATA in-memory optimized OLTP tables are more useful as transactional OLTP applications, where you would not want to lose data and transactions after SQL Server crashes or restarts.

The in-memory OLTP feature is only supported on the 64-bit Enterprise, Developer, or Evaluation editions of SQL Server 2014.

You can use the Memory Optimization Advisor wizard, which can be launched from SQL Server 2014 Management Studio, to help identify and migrate fully compatible tables in memory and select the stored procedures that can be compiled into machine code for high-performance execution.

For more information on how to use this wizard, see the *Memory Optimization Advisor* article at http://msdn.microsoft.com/en-us/library/dn284308.aspx.

The limitations of memory-optimized tables

In-memory optimized OLTP tables do not support a full set of SQL Server and Transact-SQL features that are supported by traditional, disk-based tables. Some of the key limitations of in-memory optimized OLTP tables include no support for SPARSE, IDENTITY, and computed columns; DML triggers; FILESTREAM data; columnstore, filtered, and full-text indexes; the ROWGUIDCOL option; FOREIGN KEY, CHECK, and UNIQUE constraints; TRUNCATE TABLE, MERGE, and dynamic and key set cursors.

The following data types are not supported by in-memory optimized tables: Datetimeoffset, geography, geometry, and LOBs (varchar(max), image, XML, text, and ntext).

For a full list of SQL Server 2014 features that are not supported with memory-optimized tables, see the MSDN resource *Transact-SQL Constructs Not Supported by In-Memory OLTP* at http://msdn.microsoft.com/en-us/library/dn246937.aspx.

Indexes

As a database administrator (DBA) or developer, one of your most important goals is to ensure that the query times are consistent with the **service-level agreement** (**SLA**) and are meeting user expectations. Along with other performance enhancement techniques, creating indexes for your queries on underlying tables is one of the most effective and common ways to achieve this objective.

The indexes of underlying relational tables are very similar in purpose to an index section at the back of a book. For example, instead of flipping through each page of the book, you use the index section at the back of the book to quickly find the particular information or topic within the book. In the same way, instead of scanning each individual row on the data page, SQL Server uses indexes to quickly find the data for the qualifying query. Therefore, by indexing an underlying relational table, you can significantly enhance the performance of your database.

Indexing affects the processing speed for both OLTP and OLAP and helps you achieve optimum query performance and response time.

The cost associated with indexes

As mentioned earlier, SQL Server uses indexes to optimize overall query performance. However, there is also a cost associated with indexes; that is, indexes slow down insert, update, and delete operations. Therefore, it is important to consider the cost and benefits associated with indexes when you plan your indexing strategy.

How SQL Server uses indexes

A table that doesn't have a clustered index is stored in a set of data pages called a heap. Initially, the data in the heaps is stored in the order in which the rows are inserted into the table. However, SQL Server Database Engine moves the data around the heap to store the rows efficiently. Therefore, you cannot predict the order of the rows for heaps because data pages are not sequenced in any particular order. The only way to guarantee the order of the rows from a heap is to use the SELECT statement with the ORDER BY clause.

Access without an index

When you access the data, SQL Server first determines whether there is a suitable index available for the submitted SELECT statement. If no suitable index is found for the submitted SELECT statement, SQL Server retrieves the data by scanning the entire table. The database engine begins scanning at the physical beginning of the table and scans through the full table page by page and row by row to look for qualifying data that is specified in the submitted SELECT statement. Then, it extracts and returns the rows that meet the criteria in the format specified in the submitted SELECT statement.

Access with an index

The process is improved when indexes are present. If the appropriate index is available, SQL Server uses it to locate the data. An index improves the search process by sorting data on key columns. The database engine begins scanning from the first page of the index and only scans those pages that potentially contain qualifying data based on the index structure and key columns. Finally, it retrieves the data rows or pointers that contain the locations of the data rows to allow direct row retrieval.

The structure of indexes

In SQL Server, all indexes—except full-text, XML, in-memory optimized, and columnstore indexes—are organized as a **balanced tree (B-tree)**. This is because full-text indexes use their own engine to manage and query full-text catalogs, XML indexes are stored as internal SQL Server tables, in-memory optimized indexes use the Bw-tree structure, and columnstore indexes utilize SQL Server in-memory technology.

In the B-tree structure, each page is called a node. The top page of the B-tree structure is called the root node. Non-leaf nodes, also referred to as intermediate levels, are hierarchical tree nodes that comprise the index sort order. Non-leaf nodes point to other non-leaf nodes that are one step below in the B-tree hierarchy, until reaching the leaf nodes. Leaf nodes are at the bottom of the B-tree hierarchy. The following diagram illustrates the typical B-tree structure:

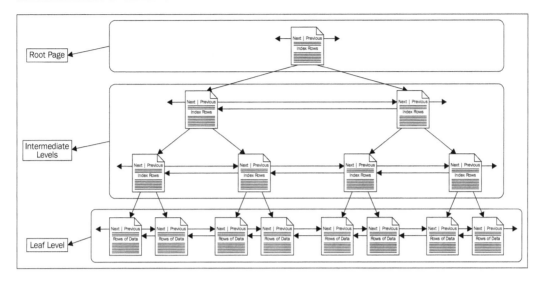

Index types

In SQL Server 2014, you can create several types of indexes. They are explored in the next sections.

Clustered indexes

A clustered index sorts table or view rows in the order based on clustered index key column values. In short, a leaf node of a clustered index contains data pages, and scanning them will return the actual data rows. Therefore, a table can have only one clustered index. Unless explicitly specified as nonclustered, SQL Server automatically creates the clustered index when you define a PRIMARY KEY constraint on a table.

When should you have a clustered index on a table?

Although it is not mandatory to have a clustered index per table, according to the TechNet article, *Clustered Index Design Guidelines*, with few exceptions, every table should have a clustered index defined on the column or columns that used as follows::

- The table is large and does not have a nonclustered index. The presence of a clustered index improves performance because without it, all rows of the table will have to be read if any row needs to be found.

- A column or columns are frequently queried, and data is returned in a sorted order. The presence of a clustered index on the sorting column or columns prevents the sorting operation from being started and returns the data in the sorted order.

- A column or columns are frequently queried, and data is grouped together. As data must be sorted before it is grouped, the presence of a clustered index on the sorting column or columns prevents the sorting operation from being started.

- A column or columns data that are frequently used in queries to search data ranges from the table. The presence of clustered indexes on the range column will help avoid the sorting of the entire table data.

Nonclustered indexes

Nonclustered indexes do not sort or store the data of the underlying table. This is because the leaf nodes of the nonclustered indexes are index pages that contain pointers to data rows. SQL Server automatically creates nonclustered indexes when you define a UNIQUE KEY constraint on a table. A table can have up to 999 nonclustered indexes.

You can use the CREATE INDEX statement to create clustered and nonclustered indexes. A detailed discussion on the CREATE INDEX statement and its parameters is beyond the scope of this chapter. For help with this, refer to the *CREATE INDEX (Transact-SQL)* article at http:// msdn.microsoft.com/en-us/library/ms188783.aspx.

SQL Server 2014 also supports new inline index creation syntax for standard, disk-based database tables, temp tables, and table variables. For more information, refer to the *CREATE TABLE (SQL Server)* article at http://msdn.microsoft.com/en-us/library/ms174979.aspx.

Single-column indexes

As the name implies, single-column indexes are based on a single-key column. You can define it as either clustered or nonclustered. You cannot drop the index key column or change the data type of the underlying table column without dropping the index first. Single-column indexes are useful for queries that search data based on a single column value.

Composite indexes

Composite indexes include two or more columns from the same table. You can define composite indexes as either clustered or nonclustered. You can use composite indexes when you have two or more columns that need to be searched together. You typically place the most unique key (the key with the highest degree of selectivity) first in the key list.

For example, examine the following query that returns a list of account numbers and names from the `Purchasing.Vendor` table, where the name and account number starts with the character A:

```
USE [AdventureWorks2012];

SELECT  [AccountNumber] ,
        [Name]
FROM    [Purchasing].[Vendor]
WHERE   [AccountNumber] LIKE 'A%'
        AND [Name] LIKE 'A%';
GO
```

If you look at the execution plan of this query without modifying the existing indexes of the table, you will notice that the SQL Server query optimizer uses the table's clustered index to retrieve the query result, as shown in the following screenshot:

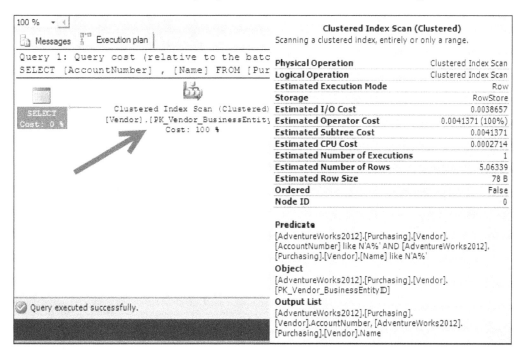

As our search is based on the `Name` and `AccountNumber` columns, the presence of the following composite index will improve the query execution time significantly:

```
USE [AdventureWorks2012];
GO


CREATE NONCLUSTERED INDEX [AK_Vendor _ AccountNumber_Name]
  ON [Purchasing].[Vendor] ([AccountNumber] ASC, [Name] ASC) ON
  [PRIMARY];
GO
```

Now, examine the query execution plan of this query once again, after creating the previous composite index on the `Purchasing.Vendor` table, as shown in the following screenshot:

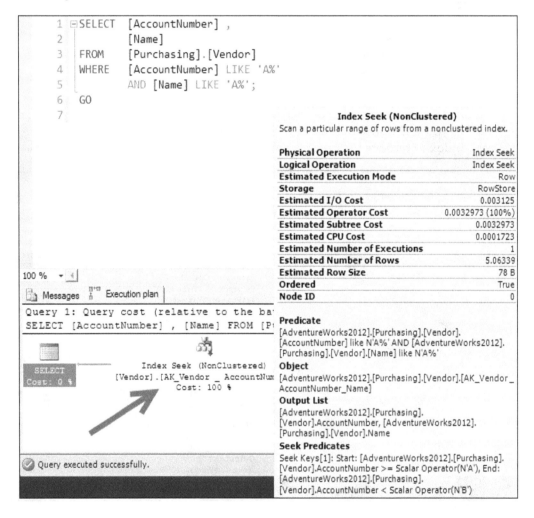

As you can see, SQL Server performs a seek operation on this composite index to retrieve the qualifying data.

Covering indexes

SQL Server 2005 introduces included columns in indexes, also known as covering indexes. Included columns are nonkey columns. Query performance improves when all columns in a query are included in the index as either key or nonkey columns. SQL Server Database Engine stores nonkey columns at the index leaf level, which is the bottommost level of the index hierarchy, and not in the index row. Included columns are supported on nonclustered indexes only. Columns included as nonkey columns have the following features:

- They are not included in the 900-byte index key limit
- They can be data types that are not allowed as key columns
- They can include computed columns, but require deterministic values
- They cannot include text, ntext, or image data types
- They cannot be used as both key and nonkey columns

For example, consider that you now want to retrieve all columns from the Purchasing.Vendor table based on the values of the Name and AccountNumber columns. To accomplish this, execute the following query:

```
USE [AdventureWorks2012];
GO

SELECT [AccountNumber]
      , [Name]
      , [CreditRating]
      , [PreferredVendorStatus]
      , [ActiveFlag]
      , [PurchasingWebServiceURL]
      , [ModifiedDate]
FROM [Purchasing].[Vendor]
WHERE [AccountNumber] IN (N'AUSTRALI0001', N'JEFFSSP0001',
N'MITCHELL0001')
   AND [Name] IN (N'Inner City Bikes', N'Hill Bicycle Center');
GO
```

Examine the execution plan of this query without modifying the existing indexes of the table; refer to the following screenshot:

You will notice that SQL Server uses the table's clustered index to retrieve the query result. This is because the query contains the columns that are not part of the nonclustered index. Therefore, SQL Server uses the clustered index to retrieve the query results. To improve this query performance, you can modify your nonclustered composite index on the `Purchasing.Vendor` table, which we created earlier, to add the remaining columns of the query as nonkey columns in this composite index. Have a look at the following code snippet:

```
USE [AdventureWorks2012];
GO

CREATE NONCLUSTERED INDEX [AK_Vendor_AccountNumber_Name]
  ON [Purchasing].[Vendor] ([AccountNumber] ASC, [Name] ASC )
INCLUDE([CreditRating]
        ,[PreferredVendorStatus]
        ,[ActiveFlag]
        ,[PurchasingWebServiceURL]
        ,[ModifiedDate]) ON [PRIMARY];
GO
```

After creating the previous composite index with included columns, run the query and examine its query execution plan as show in the following screenshot:

Unique indexes

You can use unique indexes to enforce uniqueness on the key columns. If you attempt to add rows or change data that generates duplicate data in a table that is indexed by a unique index, the operation is aborted and SQL Server reports an error. A unique index has the following features:

- It can have one or more key columns
- It can be created as a clustered or nonclustered index
- It checks for duplicate values when the index is created or rebuilt
- It checks for duplicate values during data manipulation (INSERT or UPDATE)

By default, SQL Server creates a unique clustered index when you define a primary key and a unique nonclustered index when you define a unique constraint. However, you can override the default behavior to define a nonclustered index on the primary key and clustered unique constraint. A unique index ensures the data integrity of the defined columns and provides additional information that is helpful to the query optimizer and can produce more efficient execution plans.

For more information on unique indexes, refer to the *Create Unique Indexes* article at http://msdn.microsoft.com/en-us/library/ms187019.aspx.

Spatial indexes

SQL Server supports spatial data and spatial indexes. A spatial index is an extended index that allows you to index a spatial column. A spatial column is a data table column that contains spatial data types, such as geometry or geography.

A detailed discussion on spatial indexes is beyond the scope of this chapter. For help with this, download the white paper, *New Spatial Features in SQL Server 2012*, for a detailed description and examples of the spatial feature and the effect of spatial indexes.

Partitioned indexes

Partitioned indexes are created on partitioned tables. They are partitioned on the same horizontal filter and ranges as the table that they are based on. You can specify the table partition scheme (how the table is partitioned) when creating partitioned indexes. You can also create partitioned indexes on existing nonpartitioned tables, but to do this, you first have to convert the existing nonpartitioned tables into partitioned tables. To do this, you first need to add appropriate partitioned filegroups, then create a partitioned function and partition scheme inside of the database. Once done, you need to rebuild the desired table index/indexes on this partition.

Partitioned indexes not only help optimize queries that include data only from a single partition, but they also help make index management operations easier because you can also rebuild the partition of an index that is fragmented individually.

> A detailed discussion on partitioned tables and indexes is outside the scope of this chapter. For more information, see the *Partitioned Tables and Indexes* article at http://msdn.microsoft.com/en-us/library/ms190787.aspx.

Filtered indexes

Beginning with SQL Server 2008, Microsoft introduced a new type of nonclustered index known as a filtered index. A filtered index is an optimized nonclustered index that only contains the subset of data specified by the filter predicate. Filtered indexes are especially useful to cover those queries that frequently need access to a well-defined subset of data. Having a well-designed filtered index can improve query performance, reducing the overall index maintenance costs and index storage costs compared to full-table indexes.

For example, have a look at the following query that returns all of the orders from Sales.SalesOrderDetail that are placed on or after January 1, 2008:

```
USE [AdventureWorks2012]
GO

SELECT  [SalesOrderID] ,
        [SalesOrderDetailID] ,
        [OrderQty] ,
        [ProductID] ,
        [SpecialOfferID] ,
        [UnitPrice] ,
```

```
            [UnitPriceDiscount] ,
            [LineTotal] ,
            [ModifiedDate]
    FROM    [Sales].[SalesOrderDetail]
    WHERE [ModifiedDate] >= '2008-01-01 00:00:00.000';
    GO
```

By creating the following filtered index, you can significantly improve the query response time because SQL Server will perform an index seek on this filtered index to retrieve the qualifying data:

```
USE [AdventureWorks2012];
GO

CREATE NONCLUSTERED INDEX IXNC_SalesOrderDetail_ModifiedDate
ON [Sales].[SalesOrderDetail] ([ModifiedDate])
INCLUDE ([SalesOrderID]
    ,[SalesOrderDetailID]
    ,[OrderQty]
    ,[ProductID]
    ,[SpecialOfferID]
    ,[UnitPrice]
    ,[UnitPriceDiscount]
    ,[LineTotal])
WHERE [ModifiedDate] >= '2007-01-01 00:00:00.000';
GO
```

Full-text indexes

A full-text search is a word search based on character string data. The Microsoft Full-Text Engine for SQL Server automatically creates and maintains a full-text catalog when you enable a table to do a full-text search.

For more information on full-text indexes, see the *Populate Full-Text Indexes* article at http://msdn.microsoft.com/en-us/library/ms142575.aspx.

XML indexes

XML indexes are persisted representations of the data contained in an XML data type column. They have different procedures of creation and management from standard indexes, and they are structured differently from standard indexes as well. There are two main XML index types: primary and secondary. You must create a primary index first and can then create one or more secondary indexes. When creating XML indexes, the base table must have a primary key constraint defined. If the base table is a partitioned table, XML indexes will use the same partitioning function and partitioning scheme. Moreover, you can create one primary index and one or more secondary indexes for each XML column in the base table. If you are using data type methods, you should create at least a primary index. All data type methods use the primary index for optimization if it is present.

For more information on XML indexes, see the *XML Indexes (SQL Server)* article at `http://msdn.microsoft.com/en-us/library/ms191497.aspx`.

Memory-optimized indexes

You create memory-optimized indexes on memory-optimized tables. You can only create nonclustered indexes on memory-optimized tables. The nonclustered indexes of memory-optimized tables are structured as a Bw-tree. The Bw-tree is a high-performance, latch-free B-tree index structure that exploits log-structured storage. The following diagram illustrates the Bw-tree architecture:

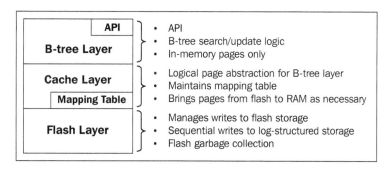

Like memory-optimized tables, memory-optimized indexes also reside in memory. You can create two types of nonclustered indexes. These are as follows:

- **Nonclustered, memory-optimized hash indexes**: These indexes are made for point lookups. They do not have pages and are always fixed in size. The values returned from a query using a hash index are not sorted. Hash indexes are optimized for index seeks on equality predicates and also support full index scans. Queries that use hash indexes return results in an unsorted order.

- **Nonclustered, memory-optimized non-hash indexes**: These are made for range scans and ordered scans. They support everything that hash indexes support, plus seek operations, such as greater than or less than, on inequality predicates as well as sort order. Queries that use non-hash indexes return results in a sorted order.

For more information on memory-optimized indexes, see the extensive set of documentation named *Introduction to Indexes on Memory-Optimized Tables* at http://msdn.microsoft.com/en-us/library/dn511012.aspx.

Columnstore indexes

SQL Server 2014 is another fascinating release, which has several compelling, performance-related features, out of which the updatable, in-memory columnstore (abbreviated to xVelocity where appropriate) index is one of them. Columnstore indexes allow you to deliver predictable performance for large data volumes. Columnstore indexes were first introduced with SQL Server 2012 to significantly improve the performance of data warehouse workloads. According to Microsoft, you can achieve up to 10x performance improvements for certain data warehousing analytical queries using in-memory columnstore indexes.

The in-memory columnstore index feature is one of the most significant scalability and performance enhancements of SQL Server 2012. However, the SQL Server 2012 implementation of in-memory columnstore indexes is not updatable, which means that you cannot perform DML operations on tables once the in-memory columnstore index is created on them. Therefore, the underlying table that you are creating the columnstore index on has to be read only. Moreover, to update data on the underlying table, you need to first drop or disable the columnstore index and then enable or recreate the columnstore index once the data in the underlying table is updated. SQL Server 2014 removed this restriction and introduced updatable in-memory columnstore indexes.

Unlike SQL Server 2012 Database Engine, which only supports nonclustered columnstore indexes, SQL Server 2014 Database Engine supports both clustered and nonclustered columnstore indexes. Both these types of SQL Server 2014 columnstore indexes use the same in-memory technology but have different purposes. The clustered columnstore indexes of SQL Server 2014 are updatable, which means that you can perform DML operations on the underlying table without having to disable or remove the clustered columnstore index.

The architecture of columnstore indexes

Unlike traditional B-tree indexes, where data is stored and grouped in a row-based fashion, the columnstore indexes group and store data for each column on a separate set of disk pages. For example, consider the following table with 8 columns:

Row 1	Col1	Col2	Col3	Col4	Col5	Col6	Col7	Col8
Row 2	Col1	Col2	Col3	Col4	Col5	Col6	Col7	Col8
Row 3	Col1	Col2	Col3	Col4	Col5	Col6	Col7	Col8
Row 4	Col1	Col2	Col3	Col4	Col5	Col6	Col7	Col8
Row 5	Col1	Col2	Col3	Col4	Col5	Col6	Col7	Col8
Row 6	Col1	Col2	Col3	Col4	Col5	Col6	Col7	Col8
Row 7	Col1	Col2	Col3	Col4	Col5	Col6	Col7	Col8
...	...	...	...	...	...	...	...	...
...	...	...	...	...	...	...	...	...
Row n	Col1	Col2	Col3	Col4	Col5	Col6	Col7	Col8

When you create the traditional B-tree index on this table, SQL Server stores multiple table rows per index page as illustrated in the following diagram:

Index Page 1

Row 1	Col1	Col2	Col3	Col4	Col5	Col6	Col7	Col8
Row 2	Col1	Col2	Col3	Col4	Col5	Col6	Col7	Col8
Row 3	Col1	Col2	Col3	Col4	Col5	Col6	Col7	Col8
Row 4	Col1	Col2	Col3	Col4	Col5	Col6	Col7	Col8
Row 5	Col1	Col2	Col3	Col4	Col5	Col6	Col7	Col8
Row 6	Col1	Col2	Col3	Col4	Col5	Col6	Col7	Col8
Row 7	Col1	Col2	Col3	Col4	Col5	Col6	Col7	Col8
Row 8	Col1	Col2	Col3	Col4	Col5	Col6	Col7	Col8
Row 9	Col1	Col2	Col3	Col4	Col5	Col6	Col7	Col8
Row 10	Col1	Col2	Col3	Col4	Col5	Col6	Col7	Col8

Index Page 2

Row 11	Col1	Col2	Col3	Col4	Col5	Col6	Col7	Col8
Row 12	Col1	Col2	Col3	Col4	Col5	Col6	Col7	Col8
Row 13	Col1	Col2	Col3	Col4	Col5	Col6	Col7	Col8
Row 14	Col1	Col2	Col3	Col4	Col5	Col6	Col7	Col8
Row 15	Col1	Col2	Col3	Col4	Col5	Col6	Col7	Col8
Row 16	Col1	Col2	Col3	Col4	Col5	Col6	Col7	Col8
Row 17	Col1	Col2	Col3	Col4	Col5	Col6	Col7	Col8
...	...	...	...	...	...	...	...	...
...	...	...	...	...	...	...	...	...
Row n	Col1	Col2	Col3	Col4	Col5	Col6	Col7	Col8

When you create the columnstore index on this table, SQL Server stores the data for each column on a separate index page as illustrated in the following diagram:

	Index Page1	Index Page2	Index Page3	Index Page4	Index Page5	Index Page6	Index Page7	Index Page8
Row 1	Col1	Col2	Col3	Col4	Col5	Col6	Col7	Col8
Row 2	Col1	Col2	Col3	Col4	Col5	Col6	Col7	Col8
Row 3	Col1	Col2	Col3	Col4	Col5	Col6	Col7	Col8
Row 4	Col1	Col2	Col3	Col4	Col5	Col6	Col7	Col8
Row 5	Col1	Col2	Col3	Col4	Col5	Col6	Col7	Col8
Row 6	Col1	Col2	Col3	Col4	Col5	Col6	Col7	Col8
Row 7	Col1	Col2	Col3	Col4	Col5	Col6	Col7	Col8
Row 8	Col1	Col2	Col3	Col4	Col5	Col6	Col7	Col8
Row 9	Col1	Col2	Col3	Col4	Col5	Col6	Col7	Col8
Row 10	Col1	Col2	Col3	Col4	Col5	Col6	Col7	Col8

A columnstore index does not physically store columns in a sorted order. Instead, it is based on VertiPaq compression technology, which allows large amounts of data to be compressed in memory. This highly compressed, in-memory store, significantly improves the query execution time by improving the buffer pool usage, while reducing the total disk I/O and CPU usage. This is because only the column-based data pages needed to solve the query are fetched from disk and moved in memory.

Creating and managing columnstore indexes

You can use the CREATE CLUSTERED COLUMNSTORE INDEX statement to create a clustered columnstore index and the CREATE COLUMNSTORE INDEX statement to create a nonclustered columnstore index. To create a clustered columnstore index, use the following code:

```
CREATE CLUSTERED COLUMNSTORE INDEX index_name
ON [database_name].[schema_name].[table_name]
    [ WITH ( <columnstore_index_option> [ ,...n ] ) ]
    [ ON {
        partition_scheme_name ( column_name )
        | filegroup_name
        | "default"
        }][ ; ]
```

To create a nonclustered columnstore index, use the following code:

```
CREATE [NONCLUSTERED] COLUMNSTORE INDEX index_name
    ON [database_name].[schema_name].[table_name]
        ( column   [ ,...n ] )
    [ WITH ( <columnstore_index_option> [ ,...n ] ) ]
    [ ON {
        partition_scheme_name ( column_name )
        | filegroup_name
        | "default"
        } ] [ ; ]
```

When creating columnstore indexes, you need to consider the following:

- The columnstore index feature is only available in the SQL Server 2014 Enterprise, Evaluation, and Developer editions.
- Columnstore indexes cannot be combined with the following SQL Server features: page and row compression, replication, filestreams, change tracking, and CDC.
- Clustered columnstore indexes must include all columns of the table.
- You cannot create columnstore indexes on other indexes or indexed views.
- Columnstore indexes cannot have more than 1,024 columns.
- Columnstore indexes cannot include sparse columns, unique constraints, primary key constraints, or foreign key constraints.
- Columnstore indexes cannot include columns with the following data types: ntext, text, image, varchar(max), nvarchar(max), varbinary(max), rowversion (and timestamp), sql_variant, CLR types (hierarchyid and spatial types), and XML.
- Avoid creating columnstore indexes on tables that are frequently updated or need small lookup queries. They are only suitable for read-mostly, read-intensive, large database tables.

You can use the ALTER INDEX statement to modify a columnstore index. You can use ALTER INDEX...REBUILD with the COLUMNSTORE_ARCHIVE data compression option to further compress the columnstore index, which is suitable for situations where the archiving of data is possible. You can use the DROP INDEX statement to delete a columnstore index.

You can also use SQL Server 2014 Management Studio to create columnstore indexes in the same way that you use it to manage standard, disk-based table indexes. For example, to create a new clustered columnstore index, in **Object Explorer**, expand table and right-click on the Indexes folder. Next, choose **New Index** and then the new clustered columnstore index.

Guidelines for designing and optimizing indexes

The following sections will cover some guidelines that you can follow to make indexes more effective and improve performance during the creation, implementation, and maintenance of indexes.

Avoid overindexing tables

Indexes are the solution to many performance problems, but too many indexes on tables affect the performance of INSERT, UPDATE, and DELETE statements. This is because SQL Server updates all indexes on the table when you add (INSERT), change (UPDATE), or remove (DELETE) data from a table. Therefore, it is recommended that you only create required indexes on the tables by analyzing the data access requirements of the application or users.

Create a clustered index before creating nonclustered indexes when using clustered indexes

As mentioned earlier, the leaf layer of a clustered index is made up of data pages that contain table rows, and the leaf layer of a nonclustered index is made up of index pages that contain pointers to the data rows. In addition, SQL Server sorts table rows in the clustered index order based on key column values, while the nonclustered index does not affect the table sort order. When we define the nonclustered index on a table first, the nonclustered index contains a nonclustered index key value and a row locator, which points to a heap that contains a key value. However, if the table has a clustered index, a leaf node of the nonclustered index points to a leaf node location in the clustered index. So, when you create or rebuild the clustered index, the leaf node structure of the nonclustered index also changes. Therefore, you need to follow this rule because the creation or changing of the clustered index will also change the nonclustered indexes of the tables.

Index columns used in foreign keys

Foreign key columns are always good candidates for nonclustered indexes because they are mostly used in JOIN operations.

Index columns frequently used in joins

Be sure to create nonclustered indexes on columns that are frequently used in JOIN operations as this will improve query performance when the JOIN operation is being performed by reducing the time required to locate the required rows in each table.

Use composite indexes and covering indexes to give the query optimizer greater flexibility

When you use composite indexes, you create fewer indexes for your queries because a composite index is defined from two or more columns from the same table. This improves the query performance because the query requires less disk I/O than the same query that uses a single column index.

Covering indexes also improve query performance by reducing the overall disk I/O because all of the data needed to satisfy the query exists within the index itself.

Limit key columns to columns with a high level of selectability

We need to limit key columns to columns with a high level of selectability because the higher the level of selectivity in a column, the more likely that it is a key column candidate. For example, good candidates for index key columns are the ones used in the DISTINCT, WHERE, ORDER BY, GROUP BY, and LIKE clauses.

Pad indexes and specify the fill factor to reduce page splits

When the database engine needs to add a row to a full index page, the database engine has to split this page to make additional space for the new row. This process of splitting pages will help keep the index hierarchy intact.

Obviously, this process is resource intensive as it depends on the size of the index and other activities in the database. The process can result in a significant loss in performance, and to prevent splits, or at least reduce the need for them, you should pad the index and specify the fill factor value. The fill factor value specifies the percentage of space on each leaf-level page to be filled with data, reserving the remainder of space for future growth. The fill factor can either be set to 0 or to a percentage between 1 and 100. The server-wide default for the fill factor value is 0, which means the leaf-level pages are filled to capacity.

A padding index leaves an open space on each page at the intermediate level of the index. The padding option in indexing is useful only when the fill factor is specified as it uses the percentage specified by the fill factor. By default, SQL Server ensures that each index page has enough space to accommodate at least one row of the maximum index size, given the set of keys on the intermediate pages. However, when you pad an index, if the percentage specified for the fill factor is not large enough to accommodate a row, SQL Server internally overrides the percentage to allow the minimum. For more information, refer to the *Specify Fill Factor for an Index* article at `http://msdn.microsoft.com/en-us/library/ms177459.aspx`.

Rebuild indexes based on the fragmentation level

Index fragmentation can occur in an active database because SQL Server maintains indexes on an ongoing basis during DML operations so that they reflect data changes. As a DBA or developer, your main goal is to look for index fragmentation and correct the fragmentation with a minimal impact on user operations.

Luckily, SQL Server provides the `sys.dm_db_index_physical_stats` dynamic management view, which you can use to detect the fragmentation in a specific index, all of the indexes in a table or indexed view, all indexes in databases, or all indexes in all databases. The `avg_fragmentation_in_percent` column of this view returns the percentage of fragmented data. Depending on the level of fragmentation, you can either rebuild or reorganize the index. For more information, see the *Reorganize and Rebuild Indexes* article at `http://msdn.microsoft.com/en-us/library/ms189858.aspx`.

Query optimization statistics

Query optimization statistics are only a form of dynamic metadata that contains statistical information about the distribution of values in one or more columns of a table or indexed view. Statistics describe index key values, are maintained for index columns, and are used by SQL Server when deciding on the most appropriate indexes to use when running queries. Statistics help estimate the cardinality, or number of rows, in the query result, and this usually helps the query optimizer make better decisions. For example, if there are only a dozen rows in a table, then there is no reason to go to the index to search. This is because it is always better to do a full table scan to find the required result set. However, if that same table grows to one million rows, then you're probably better off using the index.

The SQL Server query optimizer uses statistics to create query plans, which improves the query performance. For most queries, the query optimizer generates the necessary statistics for a high-quality query plan; in a few cases, you need to create additional statistics or modify the query design for best results.

Database-wide statistics options in SQL Server to automatically create and update statistics

There are three database-wide statistics options that you can enable to let SQL Server automatically create and manage indexes and columns statistics. These are listed as follows:

* AUTO_CREATE_STATISTICS: When this is set to ON, SQL Server automatically creates the missing statistics needed for query optimization

* AUTO_UPDATE_STATISTICS: When this is set to ON, SQL Server automatically updates the statistics as needed by the query optimizer for optimal query performance

* AUTO_UPDATE_STATISTICS_ASYNC: When this is set to ON, the SQL Server query optimizer uses asynchronous statistics updates

You can use the ALTER DATABASE Transact-SQL DDL command with the SET keyword to configure these options. Here is the general syntax for this:

```
ALTER DATABASE database_name
SET
    AUTO_CREATE_STATISTICS { ON | OFF }
  | AUTO_UPDATE_STATISTICS { ON | OFF }
  | AUTO_UPDATE_STATISTICS_ASYNC { ON | OFF }
```

By default, both AUTO_CREATE_STATISTICS and AUTO_UPDATE_STATISTICS are set to ON.

Manually create and update statistics

To create statistics, you can use the CREATE STATISTICS statement as follows:

```
CREATE STATISTICS statistics_name
ON { table|view } (column_list)
[WITH
[[ FULLSCAN | SAMPLE number PERCENT | ROWS
| STATS_STREAM = stats_stream ] [ , ] ] [ NORECOMPUTE ]]
```

To update statistics, you can use the UPDATE STATISTICS statement as follows:

```
UPDATE STATISTICS table | view [index | (statistics_name)]
[WITH [FULLSCAN | RESAMPLE | SAMPLE number PERCENT | ROWS
[[,] ALL | COLUMNS | INDEX]] [[,] NORECOMPUTE]]
```

A detailed discussion on the parameters of these two commands is beyond the scope of this chapter. For help with this, see the following articles:

- *CREATE STATISTICS (Transact-SQL)* at http://msdn.microsoft.com/en-us/library/ms188038.aspx
- *UPDATE STATISTICS (Transact-SQL)* at http://msdn.microsoft.com/en-us/library/ms187348.aspx

Determine the date when the statistics were last updated

The following two sections will cover the ways to determine when the statistics were last modified.

Using the DBCC SHOW_STATISTICS command

You can use the DBCC SHOW_STATISTICS command to retrieve the header information about the statistics. This header information also includes the data and time when the statistics were last updated. For example, the following DBCC SHOW_STATISTICS command returns information about the statistics for the AK_Employee_LoginID index of the HumanResources.Employee table in the AdventureWorks2012 database:

```
USE [AdventureWorks2012];
GO

DBCC SHOW_STATISTICS (N'HumanResources.Employee',
N'AK_Employee_LoginID');
GO
```

Using the sys.stats catalog view with the STATS_DATE() function

You can use the `sys.stats` catalog view with the `STATS_DATE()` function to view the most recent update date for each statistics object that exists for the tables, indexes, and indexed views in the database. This function accepts two parameters, that is, `object_id` and `stats_id`. To determine the date when the statistics were last updated, you need to execute the `sys.stats` system catalog view with the `STATS_DATE()` function as follows:

```
USE [AdventureWorks2012];
GO

SELECT  OBJECT_NAME([object_id]) AS [ObjectName] ,
        [name] AS [StatisticName] ,
        STATS_DATE([object_id], [stats_id]) AS
[StatisticUpdateDate]
FROM    [sys].[stats];
GO
```

The fundamentals of transactions

A transaction is a logical unit of work made up of one or more tasks. In general, a transaction is considered to have four primary characteristics: **atomicity, consistency, isolation, and durability** (**ACID**). The following is a brief explanation of these characteristics:

- **Atomicity**: The transaction is an atomic unit of work in which every task within that transaction must be completed

- **Consistency**: The transaction must leave all of the data in a consistent state

- **Isolation**: The changes made by concurrent transactions must be isolated from each other, which means that no transaction should find data in an indeterminate state (in the process of change)

- **Durability**: The changes made by the transaction are persisted

In SQL Server, the transaction log makes ACID transactions possible. This is because SQL Server first writes the transactions to the transaction log, and after that, it writes committed transactions to the data file. In the case of a system failure, SQL Server rolls back the uncommitted and rolls forward the committed transaction.

Transaction modes

SQL Server supports the following transaction modes:

- **Explicit**: The statement explicitly begins, commits, and rolls back each transaction

- **Implicit**: The next transaction begins automatically when the previous transaction commits or is rolled back

- **Autocommit**: Each statement is its own transaction

- **Batch-scoped**: All transactions that start under a **Multiple Active Result Sets** (**MARS**) session are part of a batch-scoped transaction, and any transactions not completed when the batch completes are rolled back

You can manage transactions separately for each connection. You can configure a different transaction mode for each connection as needed. Unless specified otherwise, SQL Server operates in autocommit mode with each Transact-SQL statement treated as a standalone transaction.

Implementing transactions

SQL Server supports the following statements to implement transactions.

BEGIN TRANSACTION

You can use the BEGIN TRANSACTION statement to start a new SQL Server transaction. After the transaction is opened, it stays open until it is committed or rolled back. The syntax for the BEGIN TRANSACTION statement is as follows:

```
BEGIN TRAN[SACTION] [transaction_name ]
[WITH MARK ['description']]]
```

COMMIT TRANSACTION

You can use the COMMIT TRANSACTION statement to complete the transaction. The basic syntax for the COMMIT TRANSACTION statement is as follows:

```
COMMIT [TRAN[SACTION]] [transaction_name]
```

ROLLBACK TRANSACTION

You can use the ROLLBACK TRANSACTION statement to roll back the transaction to the last savepoint or a savepoint that was specified by name. If a savepoint has not been set, the transaction rolls back to the beginning of the transaction. The basic syntax for the ROLLBACK TRANSACTION statement is as follows:

```
ROLLBACK TRAN[SACTION] [transaction_name|savepoint_name]
```

SAVE TRANSACTION

You can use SAVE TRANSACTION to establish the savepoints in a transaction. The basic syntax for this command is as follows:

```
SAVE TRAN[SACTION] savepoint_name
```

An overview of locking

Locking is a necessary part of the transaction process when working in multiuser OLTP. SQL Server uses locks to prevent update conflicts. For example, when one user is updating the data in the table, SQL Server locks prevent other users from accessing the data that is being updated. Locks help prevent the following:

- **Lost updates**: This occurs when two transactions are updating the same data simultaneously. The changes are saved to the last transaction that writes to the database, losing the changes of another transaction.

- **Dirty reads**: This occurs when a transaction reads uncommitted data from another transaction. It may lead to inaccurate changes being made to the data. This is also known as an uncommitted dependency.

- **Nonrepeatable reads**: This occurs when the row data changes between data reads. It is also referred to as an inconsistent analysis.

- **Phantoms**: This is a record that appears when a transaction rereads the data after making a change.

SQL Server can issue a lock for the following:

- **RID**: A row identifier, which locks a single row in a table
- **Key**: A key, which is a row lock within an index
- **Table**: A table, which locks all data rows and indexes

- **Database**: A database, which is used when restoring a database
- **Page**: A page, which locks an 8 KB data or index page
- **Extent**: An extent, which locks a contiguous group of pages during space allocation

 SQL Server uses dynamic lock management, which means that the level of locking can be adjusted automatically, as needed. You can refer to the dynamic management view, *sys.dm_tran_locks (Transact-SQL)*, for information on active locks at `http://msdn.microsoft.com/en-us/library/ms190345.aspx`.

Basic locks

SQL Server supports the following types of locks:

- **Shared locks (S)**: These are used when performing read-only operations against the database. Resources that are locked with a shared lock are available for the `SELECT` statement operation, but not for modification.
- **Exclusive locks (X)**: These are used for operations, such as `INSERT`, `UPDATE`, and `DELETE` statements that modify data and require exclusive locks.
- **Intent locks**: These set a lock hierarchy. The following are the types of intent locks: **intent shared (IS)**, **intent exclusive (IX)**, and **shared with intent exclusive (SIX)**.
- **Update locks (U)**: These are usually placed on a page before an update is performed. When SQL Server is ready to update the page, the lock is promoted to an exclusive page lock.
- **Schema locks**: These are used to prevent the table or index that is being used in another session from being dropped or its schema being modified. When a resource is locked with a schema lock, the object cannot be accessed.
- **Bulk update locks (BU)**: These are used to prevent other processes from accessing a table while the bulk load operation is in process.

Optimistic and pessimistic locking

The following two terms are commonly used to describe locking methods:

- **Pessimistic locking**: This locks resources as they are obtained and holds the locks throughout the duration of the transaction. Pessimistic locking is more likely to cause deadlocks. A deadlock occurs when two transactions each block access to the resources needed for the other transaction.

- **Optimistic locking**: This assumes that conflicts between transactions are not possible, but could occur. Transactions can be executed without blocking resources. The only time that the resources are controlled by a conflict is when changes are made to the data. If a conflict occurs, the transaction is rolled back.

Transaction isolation

Transaction isolation protects the transaction activities that are performed outside the transaction, meeting the isolation requirements of an ACID transaction. You can manage transaction isolation as a session-level setting that affects all operations in the sessions. You can override the isolation level for individual statements through locking options. To set the transaction isolation level, run the following code:

```
SET TRANSACTION ISOLATION LEVEL
READ COMMITTED | READ UNCOMMITTED
| REPEATABLE READ | SNAPSHOT | SERIALIZABLE
```

SQL Server 2014 supports the following transaction isolation levels:

- `READ UNCOMMITTED`: In this level, dirty reads are possible. A shared lock is not acquired, and no exclusive locks are honored.

- `READ COMMITTED`: This prevents dirty reads using shared locks or row versioning. The method used depends on the configuration of the database option, `READ_COMMITED_SNAPSHOT`. If set to `ON`, SQL Server uses row versioning. If set to `OFF`, SQL Server uses shared locks.

 Using row versioning improves concurrency because SQL Server manages row versioning at a statement level, nonrepeatable reads, which are caused by data changes between reads that might occur.

- `REPEATABLE READ`: Dirty reads and nonrepeatable reads cannot occur. Read locks are held until the transaction is committed or rolled back.

- `SNAPSHOT`: Data changes made outside the transaction after the transaction begins are not visible within the transaction. This transaction isolation level uses row versioning. No shared locks are held. When you try to update the data, SQL Server compares the current data with those stored in `tempdb`. If they are different, the update fails and the transaction is rolled back.

- `SERIALIZABLE`: Other transactions cannot update or insert any new rows that were read by the transaction until after the current transaction is committed.

SQL Server 2014 tools for monitoring and troubleshooting SQL Server performance

There are a number of tools that you can use to monitor SQL Server Database Engine performance. These are explored in the following sections.

Activity Monitor

Activity Monitor is a tool in SQL Server 2014 Management Studio that gives you a view of current connections on SQL Server. You can use it to view information about the current processes and locks held on SQL Server resources. To open Activity Monitor in SQL Server Management Studio, right-click on the SQL Server instance name in **Object Explorer** and then select **Activity Monitor**.

To find blocked processes with Activity Monitor, use the following steps:

1. First click on **Processes** in **Activity Monitor** to open the **Process Info** page.
2. Then, locate the process that is waiting, scroll over to the **Blocked By** column, and note the process ID in that column.
3. Find this process ID on the **Process Info** page.
4. If you want to terminate the blocking process, right-click on it and choose **Kill Process**.

The SQLServer:Locks performance object

You can use the SQLServer:Locks object counter in **Performance Monitor** to view current statistics or create a log or alert to monitor locks and deadlocks. For example, you can monitor statistics such as the average wait time, number of deadlocks per second, and lock timeouts per second to determine whether there is a problem with resource contention on SQL Server. The following are the steps to monitor the SQLServer: Locks performance counter:

1. On the Start menu, point to **Run**, type perfmon in the **Run** dialog box, and then click on **OK** to launch **Performance Monitor**.
2. Right-click anywhere on the screen and then choose **Add Counters....**
3. Scroll down to locate and add the following SQL Server lock counters: **Average Wait Time, Number of deadlocks/sec,** and **Locks Timeouts/sec**. Once done, click on **OK** to save the configuration.

Dynamic Management Views

SQL Server 2014 provides the following three **Dynamic Management Views** (**DMVs**) that provide detailed information about locks and blocks:

- `sys.dm_exec_requests`: You can use this to obtain detailed information about requests that are currently being executed on SQL Server

- `sys.dm_tran_locks`: You can use this to obtain information about current locks and the processes that are blocking them

- `sys.dm_os_waiting_tasks`: You can use this to view detailed information on blocked and blocking processes

SQL Server Profiler

You can use SQL Server Profiler to capture SQL Server Database Engine activities based on selected events. SQL Server Profiler includes a set of predefined templates that meet the most common trace capture scenarios. You can save the trace to file or in a SQL Server database, which will allow you to monitor the data in real time. You can also replay the trace in real time or step by step in the same or on another SQL Server Database Engine instance.

You use the SQL Server Profiler Lock event category to create a trace of events related to locks and deadlocks. The event classes you might be interested in when troubleshooting locking and blocking include the following:

- `Deadlock_Graph_Event_Class`: This creates an XML description of the deadlocks

- `Lock:Acquired`: This is used in conjunction with `Lock:Released` to determine the types of locks being requested and the length of time they will be retained for

- `Lock:Cancel`: This is used to determine which locks were cancelled

- `Lock:Deadlock`: This is used to determine the objects and applications involved in a deadlock

- `Lock:Escalation`: This reports information about locks that have been escalated to cover a larger resource, for example, when a row lock becomes a table lock

- `Lock:Released`: This is used in conjunction with `Lock:Acquired`

- `Lock:Timeout(timeout>0)`: This provides information about locks that have timed out due to blocking issues

- `Lock:Timeout`: This provides the same information as `Lock:Timeout` (`timeout>0`), but includes timeouts where the duration was 0

The sp_who and sp_who2 system stored procedures

You can use the sp_who and sp_who2 system stored procedures to return information about all of the sessions that are currently established in SQL Server.

 The blk column of sp_who and the blkby column of sp_who2 contain the spid for the blocking process.

SQL Server Extended Events

SQL Server Extended Events is an event infrastructure that is a highly scalable and lightweight performance monitoring system and uses very few system resources. Extended Events can be used to capture all SQL Server Database Engine and Analysis Services events to specific consumers, as defined in SQL Server Extended Events, through XEvents. For example, you can use SQL Server Extended Events to monitor blocks and deadlocks. The SQL Server Extended Events infrastructure is integrated directly into SQL Server and can easily be managed with Transact-SQL. For more information, see the *Extended Events* article at http://msdn.microsoft.com/en-us/library/bb630282.aspx.

Summary

In this chapter, you learned about the architecture of SQL Server Relational Engine. You also learned about SQL Server 2014 in-memory technology. You learned about SQL Server indexes and how they help achieve optimal query performance while reducing the overall response time. You got an understanding of the architectural differences between the B-tree, Bw-tree, and xVelocity columnstore indexes. You also got an idea of the purpose of SQL Server query optimization statistics. You learned about SQL Server transactions and locks. You also learned about the tools that come with SQL Server Database Engine, which you can use to monitor and troubleshoot the performance of SQL Server.

Index

CREATE TYPE
  used, for creating alias data types 23
Create View pane
  Criteria pane 108
  Diagram pane 108
  SQL pane 108
CREATE VIEW statement
  about 104
  arguments 105
  example 105
CROSS JOIN operator
  using 61
CTE
  about 50, 63
  creating 63
  structure 64
CUME_DIST function 72, 73
cursor functions 53
cursor variable
  creating 99
  example 99
  syntax 99

D

data
  accessing, with index 152
  accessing, without index 152
  deleting, from SQL Server
    database tables 88
  grouping 64
  inserting, into IDENTITY column 85
  inserting, into SQL Server
    database tables 80
  organizing 64
  pivoting 66-68
  unpivoting 66-68
  updating, in SQL Server database tables 86
database
  creating, with SSMS 2014 35
  creating, with T-SQL DDL
    statements 30, 31
  dropping, with SSMS 2014 38, 39
  dropping, with T-SQL DDL statements 35
  modifying, with SSMS 2014 37, 38
  modifying, with T-SQL DDL statements 33
database administrator (DBA) 8, 151

database design process
  about 8
  conceptual design phase 9
  implementation and loading phase 10
  logical design phase 9
  phases 8
  physical design phase 10
  requirement collection and analysis phase 8
  screenshot, for lifecycle 10
  testing and evaluation phase 10
database files, SQL Server
  primary data file 16
  secondary data file 16
  transaction log file 17
database-wide statistics options, SQL Server
  AUTO_CREATE_STATISTICS 171
  AUTO_UPDATE_STATISTICS 171
  AUTO_UPDATE_STATISTICS_ASYNC 171
Data Control Language. *See* **DCL statements**
Data Definition Language. *See* **DDL**
data flow diagrams (DFDs) 8
data integrity 14
Data Manipulation Language. *See* **DML**
  statements
Data Manipulation Language (DML) 17, 79
data normalization. *See* **normalization**
data type
  about 21
  selecting, significance 21, 22
data types, SQL Server
  URL 22
date and time functions 53
DBCC SHOW_STATISTICS command
  using 172
DCL statements
  executing 27
DDL 10, 135
DDL trigger
  about 135
  creating 135, 136
  dropping 137
  EVENTDATA function 135
  example 136
  modifying 136
DECLARE statement 98

F

G

H

I

intent locks
about 176
intent exclusive (IX) 176
intent shared (IS) 176
shared with intent exclusive (SIX) 176
intent shared (IS) lock 176
INTERSECT operator
about 58
syntax 58
IS NOT operator 51
isolation 173
IS operator 51

J

JOIN operator
about 59
inner joins 59
outer joins 60
self joins 61
syntax 59

L

LAG function
about 74
syntax 74
large object (LOB) storage 22
LAST_VALUE function 76, 77
LEAD function
about 74
syntax 75
LEFT OUTER JOIN operator
using 60
LIKE operator 51
local variable
creating 98
locking 175
locking methods
optimistic locking 177
pessimistic locking 176
locks, types
bulk update locks (BU) 176
exclusive locks (X) 176
intent locks 176
schema locks 176

shared locks (S) 176
update locks (U) 176
**logical design phase, database design
process 9**
logical filename 16
lost updates 175

M

many-to-many relationship 13
master database
about 27
system-level configuration 27, 28
mathematical functions 54
Memory Optimization Advisor article
URL 150
memory-optimized indexes
about 163, 164
guidelines, for designing 168, 169
guidelines, for optimizing 168, 169
URL, for information 164
memory-optimized tables 42
MERGE statement
arguments 90
examples 91, 92
syntax 90
using 89
metadata functions 54
model based database
creating 32
model database 28
msdb database 28
Multiple Active Result Sets (MARS) 174
multiple rows
updating 87
multiple table queries
about 55
with EXCEPT operator 57
with INTERSECT operator 58
with JOIN operator 59
with UNION operator 56
multistatement table-valued function
example 126, 127
**Multiversion Concurrency
Control (MVCC) 149**

query plan aging 148
query processor. *See* Relational Engine

R

RANK function 69
ranking functions
  about 69
  DENSE_RANK 69
  NTILE 69
  RANK 69
  ROW_NUMBER 69
RDBMS 49
READ COMMITTED transaction isolation
  level 177
READ UNCOMMITTED transaction
  isolation level 177
recovery model, database
  about 29
  bulk-logged 29
  full recovery 30
  simple 29
recursive triggers 132
referential integrity 14
Relational Database Management System.
  See RDBMS
Relational Engine
  about 143, 144
  binding 145
  improved design, in SQL Server 2014 for
    cardinality estimation 148
  optimizing, for ad hoc workloads 148, 149
  parsing 145
  plan cache, clearing manually 149
  plan caching 147
  query execution 147
  query optimization 145-147
  query plan aging 148
relationships
  about 12
  many-to-many relationship 13
  one-to-many relationship 13
  one-to-one relationship 12
Reorganize and Rebuild Indexes article
  URL, for information 170
REPEATABLE READ transaction isolation
  level 177

requirement collection and analysis phase,
  database design process 8
resource database 29
RETURN statement 103
RIGHT OUTER JOIN operator
  using 60
ROLLBACK TRANSACTION statement
  about 175
  syntax 175
row
  deleting 89
  inserting, to SQL Server
    database table 82, 83
  updating 87
ROW_NUMBER function 69
rowset functions 54
row versioning 177

S

SAVE TRANSACTION statement
  about 175
  syntax 175
scalar functions, within CATCH block
  ERROR_LINE() 139
  ERROR_MESSAGE() 138
  ERROR_NUMBER() 138
  ERROR_PROCEDURE() 139
  ERROR_SEVERITY() 138
  ERROR_STATE() 138
schema
  about 39
  listing, in SSMS 2014 40
  managing, with SSMS 2014 40
  managing, with T-SQL DDL statements 40
SCHEMA_AND_DATA in-memory
  optimized OLTP tables 150
schema locks 176
SCHEMA_ONLY in-memory optimized
  OLTP tables 150
Search Arguments (SARG) 145
secondary data file 16
second normal form (2NF) 15
securables
  permissions, denying to 47
  permissions, granting to 47
  permissions, revoking to 48

multistatement table-valued functions, syntax 128
scalar-value functions, syntax 128
viewing 130, 131
user-defined integrity 14
user-defined scalar function
creating 121-123
using 123
user-defined stored procedures 112
user-defined tables 41
user-defined table-valued function
creating 124
inline table-valued function, syntax 124
multistatement table-valued function, syntax 124
using 129

V

variables
creating 98
cursor variable, creating 99
local variable, creating 98
table variable, creating 99
using 98
Venn diagram
for UNION ALL operator 56
for UNION operator 56
views
about 104
altering, with SSMS 2014 107-109
altering, with T-SQL DDL statements 104
creating 104
creating, with SSMS 2014 104, 107, 108
creating, with T-SQL 104
creating, with T-SQL DDL statements 104
dropping, with SSMS 2014 107-109
dropping, with T-SQL DDL statements 104
uses 104
using 104
Virtual Log Files (VLFs) 19

W

WAITFOR statement 103
WHERE clause 51
WHILE statement 102

X

XML indexes
about 163
URL, for information 163

Thank you for buying
SQL Server 2014 Development Essentials

About Packt Publishing

Packt, pronounced 'packed', published its first book "Mastering phpMyAdmin for Effective MySQL Management" in April 2004 and subsequently continued to specialize in publishing highly focused books on specific technologies and solutions.

Our books and publications share the experiences of your fellow IT professionals in adapting and customizing today's systems, applications, and frameworks. Our solution based books give you the knowledge and power to customize the software and technologies you're using to get the job done. Packt books are more specific and less general than the IT books you have seen in the past. Our unique business model allows us to bring you more focused information, giving you more of what you need to know, and less of what you don't.

Packt is a modern, yet unique publishing company, which focuses on producing quality, cutting-edge books for communities of developers, administrators, and newbies alike. For more information, please visit our website: www.packtpub.com.

About Packt Enterprise

In 2010, Packt launched two new brands, Packt Enterprise and Packt Open Source, in order to continue its focus on specialization. This book is part of the Packt Enterprise brand, home to books published on enterprise software – software created by major vendors, including (but not limited to) IBM, Microsoft and Oracle, often for use in other corporations. Its titles will offer information relevant to a range of users of this software, including administrators, developers, architects, and end users.

Writing for Packt

We welcome all inquiries from people who are interested in authoring. Book proposals should be sent to author@packtpub.com. If your book idea is still at an early stage and you would like to discuss it first before writing a formal book proposal, contact us; one of our commissioning editors will get in touch with you.

We're not just looking for published authors; if you have strong technical skills but no writing experience, our experienced editors can help you develop a writing career, or simply get some additional reward for your expertise.

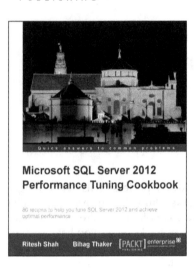

Microsoft SQL Server 2012
Performance Tuning Cookbook

ISBN: 978-1-84968-574-0   Paperback: 478 pages

80 recipes to help you tune SQL Server 2012 and achieve optimal performance

1. Learn about the performance tuning needs for SQL Server 2012 with this book and ebook.

2. Diagnose problems when they arise and employ tricks to prevent them.

3. Explore various aspects that affect performance by following the clear recipes.

Microsoft SQL Server 2012
with Hadoop

ISBN: 978-1-78217-798-2   Paperback: 96 pages

Integrate data between Apache Hadoop and SQL Server 2012 and provide business intelligence on the heterogeneous data

1. Integrate data from unstructured (Hadoop) and structured (SQL Server 2012) sources.

2. Configure and install connectors for a bi-directional transfer of data.

3. Full of illustrations, diagrams, and tips with clear, step-by-step instructions and practical examples.

Please check **www.PacktPub.com** for information on our titles

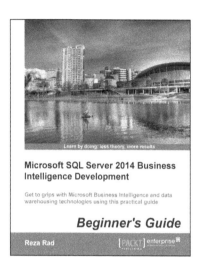

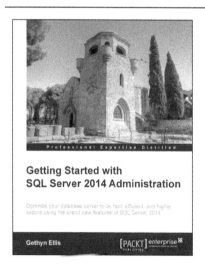

Microsoft SQL Server 2014 Business Intelligence Development Beginner's Guide

ISBN: 978-1-84968-888-8   Paperback: 350 pages

Get to grips with Microsoft Business Intelligence and data warehousing technologies using this practical guide

1. Discover the Dimensional Modeling concept while designing a data warehouse.

2. Learn Data Movement based on technologies such as SSIS, MDS, and DQS.

3. Design dashboards and reports with Microsoft BI technologies.

Getting Started with SQL Server 2014 Administration

ISBN: 978-1-78217-241-3   Paperback: 106 pages

Optimize your database server to be fast, efficient, and highly secure using the brand new features of SQL Server 2014

1. Design your SQL Server 2014 infrastructure by combining both on-premise and Windows-Azure-based technologies.

2. Implement the new InMemory OLTP database engine feature to enhance the performance of your transaction databases.

3. This is a hands-on tutorial that explores the new features of SQL Server 2014 along with giving real world examples.

Please check **www.PacktPub.com** for information on our titles

www.ingramcontent.com/pod-product-compliance
Lightning Source LLC
Chambersburg PA
CBHW060557060326
40690CB00017B/3737